NATURAL
TO MY SOUL
A PRACTICAL GUIDE FOR SELF-DISCOVERY, HEALING, AND HEALTH

By Roseanne Danielle Gault
Copyright ©2002

D1453878

Dedication

This book is dedicated to the memory of Dr. Mishra.

Acknowledgements:

I wish to show my appreciation to the following people.
To Dr. Mishra who was (and still is) a blessed guru --
thank you for being in our lives.
To Diana Wedge, without her I would never have
completed this book.
To Bill, my beloved husband, whose support is
unparalleled in all the things I do.
To our children -- our true teachers -- thanks for your
love, your life lessons, and your blessings.
To other friends who took the time to read this
manuscript and provide me with feedback.

Thanks -- OM SHANTI.

TABLE OF CONTENTS

Chapter 1. Awakening Demonstrates how a crisis can awaken a person out of their unconscious patterns and set them on the path to self-discovery.

Chapter 2. Fears Keep Us Separated Describes how our fears can keep us in the same place and reinforce our negative, recurring, and mostly unconscious patterns.

Chapter 3. Starting With the Basics Provides a framework for understanding and working with the elements that comprise life and make up our Personal Soul Psychology -- the elements of Air, Fire, Water, and Earth. Following the framework of each element's profile is:
- a 'struggle' story illustrating how easy it is to get stuck and how the 'struggle' points the way to awakening
- an analysis of the process of holism
- exercises for developing each element.

Chapter 4. The Element of Air - ATTENTION
Chapter 5. The Element of Fire - VIGILANCE
Chapter 6. The Element of Water - REFLECTION
Chapter 7. The Element of Earth - DISCERNMENT

Chapter 8. Become Your Own Sage Additional insights and strategies for increasing awareness.

Chapter 9. What is Yoga? A summary of Yoga by Dr. Ramamurti S. Mishra, M.D.

INTRODUCTION

Natural to My Soul is written for the spiritual seeker as a guide for self-discovery, healing, and health. The book provides a practical soul psychological framework for understanding and working with the elements of Air, Fire, Water, and Earth. These four basic elements of life assist the seeker in:

a. understanding their personal strengths and gifts
b. gaining clarity of the reasons behind their struggles
c. providing tools and insights on their pathway to holism and health.

By understanding your personal tendencies and what is natural to your soul, you can work objectively with the mind-body as expressions of energy, elements, and earthly matter that provide you with a vehicle for expressing your soul's purpose. Your soul is your inner essence, your inner memory, and your inner desires that struggle to be fulfilled in service to human kind. Your soul works with the body and the mind to rekindle a conscious spiritual connection to your material self. The tools for awakening to this connection are the very tools of the material self -- Air, Fire, Water, and Earth. As you work through this book and complete the exercises on each mind-body element, you will be able to follow a step-by-step approach for accessing and gaining clarity of what is natural to your soul's expression and purpose. The framework and exercises in this book draw on the understandings of Yoga and Ayurvedic wisdom. The wisdom of Yoga and Ayurveda, often referred to as 'the science of life', originated over four thousand years ago in India from wise people referred to as Rishis.

Ayurvedic knowledge says that everything on this planet is composed of five basic elements, which are Ether, Air, Fire, Water, and Earth. These elements represent five qualities of energy or matter that we use in our physical, mental and emotional lives. The qualities of these elements are diverse, dynamic, and expressive. This dynamic diversity creates the tension that provides us with energy to conduct the dance of life. By applying four of the five basic elements to understanding our lives, we see the distribution of these elements as inherently different in each of us.

By recognizing the expressions of the elements in the personal soul psychological framework, the seeker will find a practical and systematic approach for integrating the material, mental, and spiritual worlds and achieving the pursuit of holism they are craving. The framework addresses how these qualities can set in motion your challenges -- these challenges are the vehicles for awakening higher levels of awareness in the seeker and providing road signs or path markers along the way to assisting the seeker in understanding the journey itself.

PATH MARKERS

For understanding the journey through life, a number of 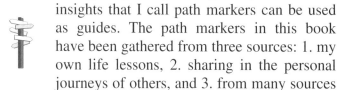 insights that I call path markers can be used as guides. The path markers in this book have been gathered from three sources: 1. my own life lessons, 2. sharing in the personal journeys of others, and 3. from many sources and wonderful teachers that I have been privileged to know. I was especially privileged to know, and be a student of, Dr. Ramamurti S. Mishra, an Indian Yogi who was among other things, a medical doctor, an endocrinologist, and a Sanskrit scholar. The road sign icon identifies the path markers found at the end of each elemental section.

MENTAL EXERCISES

Mental exercises for working with each awareness or element will be identified by the "walking shoes" icon. To tap into and draw on our strengths for problem solving requires understanding our natural tendencies and preferences. Once we know what to look for in terms of identifying our natural tendencies, then we can see what Dr. Carl G. Jung, the famous Swiss Psychiatrist, meant when he said that what appears to be random behaviour in people, once we know what to look for, is quite consistent over time. The mental exercises are designed for working with each awareness and how each awareness can assist us in making decisions about the world around us.

YOGA POSTURES (ASANSA)

A Yoga pose icon is used to identify exercises for working with our energy system at the metaphysical levels for healing and health. As the elements in the soul psychological framework are associated with Ayurvedic knowledge and this knowledge in turn is associated with Yoga philosophy, we can use the understanding of Yoga Chakras, a term which means "wheels of consciousness", for addressing and giving meaning to our evolving process. The Yoga postures along with the Yoga Chakra system for analyzing our spiritual process can help us understand and enliven the process of self-awareness. Becoming consciously aware of our mind-body tendencies, how we see our life, and how we fit into the greater scheme of things around us is what gives life its deeper meaning. Once we have this clarity, we become increasingly conscious of our natural and unique gifts, individuality, creativity and how to direct our energies for fulfilling our mission on Earth. It is my hope that this book will assist others in increasing their conscious awareness of the pursuit of holism by developing and strengthening what is natural to their soul.

CHAPTER ONE
Awakening

Tied mainly to the material physical world of subjective reality where everything we do and the results we create are mainly from our unconscious patterns, our journey to discover what's natural to our soul begins.

My first husband, David, died in a car accident in 1973. I was twenty-seven years old. We had two daughters, Stephanie who was five years old and Kathleen, two. The structure and fabric of our lives consisted for David and me of a small one-company town in upper New York State. Although we were born Catholic and were family-oriented, we were not above flirting and fooling around with others. I look back on this time of my life and wonder how we could have been so unaware of honoring our monogamous commitment to each other, our marriage, and our religion. Somehow, we managed to fool around on Saturday night and feel pious during Sunday morning mass. Although there was always gossip when people stepped outside the expected paradigms of our small town social fabric, most of us satisfied our own desires and worried about consequences only" if we got caught."

David's death marked the ending of the constraints of that social fabric for me and the beginning of a journey into an unknown but emerging personal and societal fabric.

Because the tapestry of this emerging fabric was not yet fully woven but was in the early stages of emerging, I had to define my experience from a yet unknown context and search for new symbols to represent my world. Catholicism, family constraints, living in a small town, and limited roles as a woman would no longer contain me. I began a pursuit to understand myself, my world around me, and how to make sense of both. This pursuit to define myself and to find a way to string events together and create a new fabric of understanding and meaning became a divine restlessness that has never disappeared. To live a life without this restlessness is a sleepy life. Restlessness and struggling to increase self-awareness promotes dynamism in one's dance of life. My dynamic dance of life increased during other confusing events. President Nixon was being impeached for using criminal methods to spy on his competition. Women's liberation movements were expressing hostility about male-domination, soldiers were being killed in Viet Nam and Americans were rebelling against the government for involving us in this useless war. Struggling to deal with my reactions to David's death without the structured backdrop of spouse, church, or family made me feel raw, vulnerable, and afraid. Social mores were changing. We went from suppressed or covert sexual patterns to open sexual expression; from blind patriotism to demonstrations; from cigarettes and alcohol to recreational drugs; women's liberation instead of passive compliance; changes in family roles in place of cookie-cutter patterns where men were the breadwinners and women where expected to be stay-at-home Moms; equality and diversity in the workplace in place of male domination; computer technology and the increase in the flow of information added to the physically turbulent outer world triggering and exacerbating an emotionally turbulent inner world.

TRYING TO UNDERSTAND

In the many years of pursuing an understanding of life and attempting to develop and understand how to strengthen and utilize my human potential, I began to see patterns repeating themselves in various systems of understanding human nature and our search for meaning. Many systems seem to explain how to find meaning by saying, *"look within."* But look for what? Most spiritual development systems point to self-understanding. *Physician Know Thyself* is one example. Jung's psychological theory, as another example, looks at inherent preferences for understanding mental functions. Jung encourages us to become aware of our dominant preference in order to have this preference be the captain of our ship steering us along our journey in ways that make sense to us.

No matter where I looked or with whom I studied, basic human expressions seem to influence our thoughts, our feelings, and ultimately what we did with our lives. These basic human expressions shape our lives and assist us in self-actualization when we tap into them consciously. When operating without conscious awareness of these expressions, we fall into the trap of being driven by the senses, which brings us either pain or pleasure. Driven by the senses creates a life of being tossed about on the waves of disappointments and happiness. One moment we are up and the next we are down. Unhappiness and disappointment are inevitable. Using a cognitive approach to self-development, we can seek to fully integrate and develop ourselves in meaningful ways. Objective frameworks and some basic insights and tools can give us a sense of focus, direction, and activities to pursue.

A NEW PARTNER -- ANOTHER PHASE OF LIFE

Using the framework of Yoga for understanding our journey, in our ongoing search for meaning and looking for teachers, insights and tools, my second husband, Bill and I were excited about going to India. Here we wanted to expose ourselves more deeply to the Yoga way of life. Bill and I met in 1974 and were married in 1975. Bill was already a meditator and once I learned to meditate, I was hooked on the spiritual life and Yoga as a practice for developing that lifestyle. Because of our interest in Yoga and the spiritual life, Bill and I could not wait to get to Rishikesh at the base of the Himalayas where holy people lived. In 1985, we finally arrived at Rishikesh very early one morning.

Entrance to the temples in Rishikesh, India

The overnight bus journey was rather rough. Chickens, goats, and people crowded into the bus. We already felt low, feeling somewhat disgusted by the filth and poverty of India and being tired did not help. Dropped off at a central area in Rishikesh, the scene looked as it might have a thousand years earlier. Deep within a cavern, there was a fire with men sitting around. The dawn was breaking and we truly felt like foreigners in a foreign land. With our *"Lonely Planet Survival Kit"* book in our hands, we looked around to gain our bearings and asked one of the men how to find our hotel. Although quite exhausted, we delayed going to the hotel so we could put our feet into the river, Ganges. Hindus and people who practice Yoga recognize the Ganges as a very holy river. The river was filthy and our western minds struggled against good hygienic habits as we gingerly dipped our feet into the water.

Danielle putting her foot in the Holy River, Ganges, in Rishikesh, India

Later in the day, after we walked up a small hill leading out of Rishikesh, found our hotel, and settled into our concrete slab room with two single beds and mosquito netting, we walked back down the hill looking for one of the more famous ashrams. An ashram is a place where people gather for spiritual growth. We found the ashram we were looking for and managed to get there in time for evening meditation. We both felt flat as we sat in meditation; it seemed there was no energy or magic in the room for us. Disappointed after an hour of meditation, we left the group and started walking back to our accommodations up the hill. We were very discouraged with India and I said to Bill, *"We won't make it if we don't change our mind set. Everything here is looking ugly and we have four more weeks to go. We have to turn this around."* No sooner had I said this and Bill agreed, when a young Yogi named Bala Krishna mysteriously walking up the hill stepped out of the dark night and handed us a flyer inviting us to meditation in the morning. We were delighted and felt that things would begin to turn around.

The next morning we went to breakfast and were asked to sit at a table with another couple because the dining room would soon be filled with children coming into Rishikesh from a mountain ashram. The couple we sat with consisted of an American woman called Shanti who was from Oregon and an older man called Omji from the nearby town of Deradun. During breakfast, we talked about our interest in the spiritual life and Shanti, a zealous seeker of Yoga truths, informed us of a man, who in her opinion was the last real saint in Rishikesh. She offered to take us to him after lunch. We went to our morning meditation with Bala Krishna feeling much better about India.

After lunch, we met our new Yoga friend and followed her up a steep hill to a cave. The rocks of the cave were smeared with dried cow dung where the local saint lived. Bill and I had on blue jeans and Bill was carrying a camera over his shoulder. Our minds became very busy: *What are we doing here? We have a guru in New York State. Does this mean we'll have to come to India from now on?* We both felt embarrassed as if this saint were a local tourist attraction. We sat down on the ground around a fire and then a German disciple receiving a message from the saint, told us that he was feeling tired today and did not feel like having company. Perhaps we could come back at seven, tomorrow morning. We said, *"Thank you"*, and left. Relieved to be off the hook, we questioned our motive for returning the next morning. Nevertheless, we got up early and walked to the cave to meet the saint. We sat outside the cow dung cave and waited. The German woman appeared and requested that we come back once the sun was higher, at about ten o'clock. We went off again. This time when we returned to the cave at ten o'clock, we had no doubt in our minds that we wanted to meet this saint and gain some spiritual wisdom from him.

We stepped into his cow dung cave and sat down. The interpreter asked if we had any questions. I said that my meditations were quite strong and wondered if he had any suggestions for me. He then, through the interpreter, requested that we come back and meditate by the Ganges three days in a row from eleven to noon each day. We explained that we had plane reservations and were leaving the next day but would see if we could change our plans. We understood from our Yoga training that when a guru makes a request, it is a special thing and should be honored. With the help of Omji, our local expert on how to get just about anything, we managed to change our flights. Feeling quite pleased that we could fulfill the request, we returned to the cave to receive our instructions. Each day we sat and meditated by the Ganges and on the third day of meditation, Bill and I had a similar experience toward the end of our last hour. A sensation of a visual light descended on us. We both experienced feelings of clarity, peacefulness, and gentle-hearted hugs from an intangible source. Questions disappeared. Effort was gone. We met with the saint again and mentioned our experience of light. He told us to remember this experience and to think of it whenever we wanted to feel that peace. Peace is always there in the background of our lives if we take time to reflect. As the background of life is always there, it is always available to us. The experience of a world beyond the mind and body, but fulfilled through the mind and body while in the world, comes through a clear, quiet mind. We simply have to take the time to be still and be the "being" who has an occasional "human" experience instead of a "human" who has the occasional "being" experience.

THE GOAL OF HOLISM

Ancient sages taught that the pursuit of self-knowledge and self-discovery could help people understand why they continue to get sick or stuck in repeated patterns of living. Whether thousands of years ago or today, the pursuit of holism is for people looking beyond the mundane activities of living for a deeper meaning of life. Holism comes from Ayurveda and is thought to be a complete system of natural psycho-physical-spiritual health care. The goal of holism is to ensure that the mind, body and spirit form an integral whole. The body and mind are seen as instruments for spiritual expression and when tapped into, that expression heals, strengthens, and promotes positive effects in the individual.

Spirit is defined by many terms such as life force, prana, ki, chi, or vital energy. Our objective in pursuing holism is to ensure that that vital energy, or spirit, is consciously accessible and is utilized for the betterment of all. Through various practices such as meditation, Yoga postures, conscious attention to lifestyle patterns, awareness of our actions and thoughts and their subsequent benefits or consequences, along with our interest in serving self and others, we can create positive and constructive opportunities for growth.

THE VERY ESSENCE OF LIFE

Yoga philosophy speaks of seven subtle energy centers referred to as Chakras, or energy wheels of consciousness, metaphysically positioned in the human body around the spinal column. Often associated with endocrine glands, these Chakras, or energy wheels, represent seven basic consciousness centers that provide insights into our life lessons that we encounter on our journey to holism. Supposedly, the kundalini sakti or "coiled power" within the central nervous system lies latent in the lumbar-sacral spinal region of an individual. When stimulated and awakened through postures and meditation practices, this coiled power works upward toward the top of the head, which is referred to as the Crown Chakra. Through a series of actions and reactions, the activation process of the Chakras give progressive opportunities for evolving toward the development of a person's fullest potential for self-actualization.

Once this energy is established at the top of the head, or Crown Chakra, the enlightened person can draw on the finer and finer expressions of energy establishing a flow into the physical body creating an open circuitry or loop of energy from above to below. This flow allows the person to have more than just the experience of pain-pleasure and they can now experience perfect harmony with themselves and the world around them.

THE TENSION OF OPPOSITES AND WHAT IS NATURAL TO MY SOUL

It appears we live on a planet where opposites exist and the play of opposites pulls us in opposing directions. Think about terms such as Yin and Yang, male or female, good or bad, pain or pleasure, light or dark. Dr. Jung felt that we are forced in life to decide on our inherent mental functions through opposing forces of how we take in and make decisions about information. He said we either focus more on the trees or more on the forest. We either make more subjective decisions or more objective decisions. We do both, of course, but we prefer one more than the other - one is, therefore, more natural to us and these opposing functions force us to make distinctions about ourselves. In making these distinctions about how we operate in the world around us, we become clearer about our natural gifts and what is more natural to our soul.

Opposing forces in Yoga are referred to as the male and female energies often called the Ida and the Pingala, which metaphysically flow along the opposite sides of the spinal column. These opposing energies create the tension required to activate the kundalini sakti or coiled energy at the base of the spine. The male energy is metaphysically represented as electricity and is thought of as the Father. The female energy is metaphysically represented as magnetic and is thought of as the Mother. This dynamic interplay of our male and female energy creates the tension within us forcing us to constantly strive to harmonize these same two opposing forces in order to become enlightened. The tension of opposites Jung says is the very essence of life itself. He said without the tension of opposites within us, there would be no good psychological growth. Without psychological growth, developing a conscious awareness of *"who we are or who we are not"* would leave us in a primitive state without discernment and at the mercy of nature's whims going from sense stimulation to sense stimulation.

ENERGY TRANSFORMATIONAL CENTERS

The dynamic interplay of energies expresses itself in distinctive ways once our Chakra spinal pathways are activated. Enlightenment is established in the practicing Yogi as the tension and struggles of opposing forces awaken us out of the sleepy relative world into the fully developed, integrated, and absolute expression of energy and life. The journey of awakening begins for most of us at the four lower Chakras, which link us to the material world of pain and pleasure in order for us to make our own distinctions about who we are. Here we experience ourselves through our life lessons thus stimulating in us a desire to 'awaken'.

THE FOUR LOWER CHAKRAS

Each of the four lower Chakras is related to a certain region of the body and is responsible for physiological and psychological aspects of our nature. The four lower Chakras are:

Anahata Chakra

Manipura Chakra

Svadhisthana Chakra

Muladhara Chakra

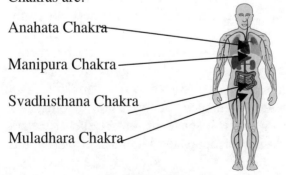

1. **MULADHARA:** *The Motivation and Life Lesson associated with this center is Security or Safety Issues* — We experience our personal soul psychological journey by being grounded in the physical form of matter. At the Muladhara center residing at the base of the spine, the Earth element dominates our consciousness as we struggle to deal with our ability to understand our place in the world and our need for survival and security. At this level, we are dependent on others for our needs. Until we are established in being a focused instrument of spiritual expressions, our survival instincts can take over as we automatically react in a flight or fight mechanistic response.

2. **SVADHISTHANA:** *The Motivation and Life Lesson associated with this center is Co-operation or Affiliation Issues* — At the second center of consciousness, the Svadhisthana, the Earth element is softened by the Water element and we begin recreating ourselves by building relationships and becoming co-dependent on others for satisfying our social and sexual needs. We begin to move beyond just the physical body's need for food and shelter. Co-habitating and sexual interests are stimulated at this center and feelings of joy, jealousy, or a desire to possess someone can create lessons in how to affiliate and co-operate with others.

3. **MANIPURA:** *The Motivation or Life Lesson associated with this center is Power or Will Issues* At the third Chakra, the Manipura center of consciousness strives to remind us of our individuality and deals with our Fire element and our will. Our sense of power and need for independence dominates our awareness as we strive to be

recognized for our unique talents. As we define our distinct personalities, we can appear to be selfish and competitive. We strive to satisfy our own needs while learning how to live in a world where others are striving to satisfy their needs.

4. **ANAHATA:** *The Motivation and Life Lesson associated with this center is Compassion, Understanding, and Spiritual Growth Issues* At the fourth Chakra known as the Anahata center, the element of Air strives to balance the three Chakras below the heart with the three Chakras above the heart. This center provides a major link to the fifth element known as Ether. Ether is made up of the union of the other four elements and connects us with the highest spiritual power that permeates the universe. Our tendency at the Heart Chakra, or the Anahata center, is to strive for balance on all levels -- to find the middle way which can lead to the cessation of suffering. Here we strive to control our emotional disturbances and our negativity. Here we become aware of our actions and the cause and effect of our actions on others. Here we begin to develop and act on right understanding and right thought as we strive to be objective yet compassionate with every living being.

BEYOND DUALISM AND CONDITIONAL MIND
THE THREE UPPER CHAKRAS

Beyond the basic elements of Air, Fire, Water, and Earth, the four elements of the individual are transformed through the higher Chakras.

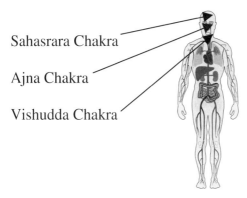

Sahasrara Chakra

Ajna Chakra

Vishudda Chakra

5. **VISHUDDA:** At the throat, refined to their purest essence, the four elements of Air, Fire, Water, and Earth dissolve into Ether. At this level of awareness, expression of knowledge is evidenced as the individual strives to overcome the struggles of the individual body-mind and the soul begins to shine forth seeking truth for truth's sake. Here the practicing Yogi moves beyond the dualistic patterns of the personality. *"The transformation of the personality through the merging and binding together of the noble and base elements, the conscious and unconscious... the conflict of opposites is transcended and the Self emerges as the centerpoint of a new harmony.[1]"* Here we develop right speech.

6. **AJNA:** In the middle of the forehead lies the sixth center called the Ajna Chakras. Here the Yogi is now beyond the five gross elements of Ether, Air, Fire, Water, and Earth. The Yogi now has unlimited power because they are at the point of non-duality during all actions. The third eye of this center is positioned

---

[1] Dr. C. G. Jung, Two Essays on Analytical Psychology, trans. By H. G. , & C. F. Baynes,Dodd,

between the two physical eyes of the past and the present and now the individual can envision the future. A feeling of oneness and unity with universal laws is experienced and the person realizes their immortality through the soul while in the mortal physical body. Here we develop right action and right livelihood.

7. **SAHASRARA:** The seventh center at the crown of the head is called the Sahasrara Chakra and represents the essence of Being. It is here that the individual self is dissolved and the higher Self, or clearest expression of awareness, is realized. Divinity within the Self is expressed as truth-being-bliss, which is English for the Yoga Sanskrit term of "sat-chit-ananda." Here we achieve right effort and right mindfulness, which leads to right meditation.

These seven centers provide us with an understanding of how to use our struggles to develop the human instrument for use on our Yoga path. Buddha, born in the sixth century BC, sought to resolve the struggles of life. He said all life is suffering and the cause of our suffering is the constant pull of our attractions and our aversions. We can cure our human suffering, he said, by eradicating the root of our misery through the practice of Yoga. The practice of Yoga helps us to develop right understanding, right thought, right speech, right action, right livelihood, right effort, right mindfulness, and right meditation. Through this practice, we develop equanimity -- the middle road.

THE YOGA CHAKRA SYSTEM

LOCATION	COLOR	FUNCTION	BALANCED	UNBALANCED	ELEMENT
CROWN OF HEAD SAHASRARA	MAGENTA	FINER INTELLECT	MEDITATION CALMNESS CLARITY	STRESSED WORRIED FEARFUL INSOMINA IRRITABLE	SPACE
FOREHEAD AJNA	PURPLE	CONSCIENCE	CONCENTRATION	FEEL OFF-BALANCED POOR CONCENTRATION LOSS OF EQUILIBRIUM	ENERGY
THROAT VISHUDDHA	BLUE	PURITY	PURIFICATION OF OUR EXPRESSIONS	POOR FACILITATION OF BREATH	ETHER
CHEST ANAHATA	GREEN	UNDERSTANDING COURAGE COMPASSION HUMILITY SELF-ACTUAL-IZATION	MIXTURE OF OUTER AND INNER ATMOSPHERES FOR WARMING AND CALMING	CONGESTION COWARDLINESS	AIR
SOLAR PLEXUS MANIPURA	YELLOW	EMOTIONAL FORCE WILL POWER	CHURNING OF THE INNER PROCESSES FOR REFINEMENT	POOR METABOLISM POOR INDIGESTION	FIRE
LOWER ABDOMEN REPRODUCTIVE SVADISTHANA	ORANGE	EMOTIONAL REACTIONS HARMONY CREATIVITY AFFILIATION	BLENDING OF ALL ELEMENTS	POOR CIRCULATION POOR RELATIONSHIPS	WATER
COCCYX SACRAL MULADHARA	RED	SECURITY SHELTER SURVIVAL	BINDING OF ALL ELEMENTS FOUNDATION STABILITY	SKELETAL-MUSCULAR PROBLEMS	EARTH

THE GOAL OF YOGA

As we awaken, our energies are activated and established upwards toward the higher Chakras. The male and female energies are united and the Yogi's Body-Mind-Spirit identifies itself with Supreme Consciousness referred to as "Brahman Bhavanam."

This is the goal of the spiritual aspirant, which is succinctly expressed as the outcome for the Jewish mystic. *"The role of the body is to facilitate the journey and fulfillment of the soul in this life, and the role of the soul is to overcome the glaring distractions of this life so that they do not distort its purpose and reality. The Torah thus urges a lifestyle in which the physical drives and impulses are channeled toward the fulfillment of the soul. At the same time, the fulfillment of the soul can never be attained at the neglect of the body or by total separation from the material".* [2]

---

[2] Gershon Winkler, The Soul of the Matter, Judaica Press, New York, 1992, p. 6.

CHAPTER TWO
FEARS KEEP US SEPARATED

Staying connected mainly to the relative world of the senses, which is driven by pain and pleasure, we will repeatedly experience the same life lessons.

For thousands of years, Eastern traditions have believed there is an energy system that is interconnected and links everything to everything else. Dr. Jung refers to one interconnection as the collective unconscious while other fields of science refer to our connection with our ancestors and our inherent characteristics through DNA. On the planetary level, an ecosystem describes the effect of changes in one area of the system on the system as a whole. We are awakening to the truth of our interconnections. In the workplace, in our homes, in our communities, and in our countries, we are experiencing the impact of our individual decisions on the planetary family as a whole. We are becoming increasingly aware that we are all connected to this one living system.

In the pursuit of holism and taking the thought that we are all interconnected, we see that our lack of awareness of our connection comes from our fears and our attachments to our beliefs and expectations triggered in the expressions of the four lower Chakras. For example, if I expect my co-workers to include me in discussions that involve me and they fail to do so, I might start to harbor resentment and start to withdraw my attention and participation with them from future work. This decision on my part will cause the relationship to deteriorate further and eventually I might either have to leave the department or find some way to retaliate as the resentment can only grow unless I do something else with my feelings.

Our fears and attachments are, however, important pieces of information which can provide clues to life's lessons if we strive to understand these clues. These clues to life's lessons come through our sensate experience in the physical body. These sensate experiences are designed to force us to reconsider, to review, and to give us a conscious choice to program how we think, feel and act. In the case of my relationship with my co-workers, the best action I can take is not to avoid or deny my feelings of resentment but to recognize them and to do something constructive with these feelings. In this example, I would try to clarify the situation by bringing it to my co-workers' attention and inquiring why I was not invited to participate. This requires courage on my part but if I hold back due to fear of what I might learn, I will end up in the same place anyway – wanting to leave my co-workers. If I continue to feel resentment toward my colleagues, this resentment will trigger a misalignment of energy in my own body, which will eventually manifest itself as some physical imbalance.

If I do attempt to clear up the misunderstanding, chances are I may find out it was either an oversight or else my co-workers were planning a surprise party on my behalf. In either case, my worrying about the situation is a waste of time. If they were out to sabotage me, it would be better for me to discover it sooner than later. At least I would not be harboring resentment for long and would be taking constructive steps to address the situation allowing me to consciously make a choice about how to proceed.

HOW TO USE THE ENERGY TIED
TO OUR FEARS

We must become more conscious of our fears and we must surface the energy tied to the "fear" content. By bringing the content to a cognitive level, we can use this energy for making choices that are more humanitarian. We can not make better choices until we are conscious of what drives us. Meeting our struggles head on and gaining clarity of the lessons in the struggles are the basis for releasing and integrating the energy tied up in our fears. Our struggles are designed to awaken us and to force us into greater awareness about our use of our own energy. The first place our bodies try to send us wakeup messages is in the physical body. We feel things such as anger, resentment, hatred, sadness, grief, satisfaction, pleasure, compassion, empathy, sympathy, peace, happiness, excitement, jealousy, disappointment. This body is the awakening tool striving to let us know when one of our Chakra centers is enlivened. At the base of the spine our attention is on security and survival needs and when threatened by my co-workers, my body sends me feelings of resentment as I fear I might be abandoned by my group. As my resentment and mistrust grows, I may start to act on these feelings which causes me to distrust them even more as I continue to create pictures of how awful "these people" are in my head. I may even find other comrades with whom to share my unhappiness. *"I'll show them that they can't do this to me,"* may be the conversation with revenge as my motivation driving my behaviours for retaliation. And on and on the drama goes -- building more walls and creating more poison in the world. A simple story but one that is written over and over again on a daily basis in many offices, departments, and families.

ATTENTION, VIGILANCE, REFLECTION, AND DISCERNMENT

A war resistance museum in Grenoble, France reminds us of what can happen when we unconsciously and blindly follow expressions of hatred. We kill people because we fear them and do not see them as part of our humanity. We project our fears onto others and in our attempt to rid ourselves of these fears, we fight to conquer our 'enemies'. Nazi Germany killed innocent people because of a vision for "a superior race." This war museum has vivid images reminding us of the struggles the Resistance went through to regain their freedom during WWII. As we near the end of the museum, we see four pillars with current video images of active hatred and what can happen when we allow our hatred to motivate our behaviours. The four pillars have the following words on them: Attention, Vigilance, Reflection, and Discernment. Unconscious patterns of hatred are instinctive in us and are inherently designed to protect us from strangers whom we perceive as potentially dangerous. However, without understanding our fears, we will keep falling down the same dark holes of misunderstanding repeating the same problems and continuously finding ourselves in the same place -- unenlightened.

Back in the eighties Bill and I attended EST seminars (Erhart's Seminar Training). These seminars were for people who wanted to "wake up" and the idea behind the seminars was to blast the ego. We were expected to react to structure while the seminar leaders kept trying to provoke us into reacting. Once people got angry with the seminar leaders, then the processing of "attitude" data began. This anger was a powerful way to show us how our reactions kept us in the same place. Following the basic EST training which took place over a full weekend, people could continue to "awaken" by attending various evening sessions. One session we attended dealt with FEAR. In the FEAR workshop we went through an exercise entitled THE FEAR EXERCISE. We formed a circle and hunching over with our heads lowered, we were told to perceive the other people in the circle as dangerous. The interesting part of the exercise was that fear became an entity, a presence in the room, and this presence seemed to exist and feed on its own force. All of us instinctively began to operate out of fear of the others. A heavy atmosphere continued to blanket the room. Then, someone giggled. Gradually we all began to giggle and then break out into laughter as we all realized that if I was feeling threatened by everyone in the circle, I was also threatening them. Our perceptions drove our feelings and our feelings where causing us to take positions about our behaviours.

When we realize that perceptions and feelings provide us with feedback, we can make choices about our responses to the feedback before we act. We have outgrown the forms our fears have worked with in the past. We need to expand our social software if we want to constructively contribute to the worldwide global village we live in today. In order to operate in today's world, our minds need to expand as the "fear" response alone is no longer a viable program by which to manage our evolutionary processes. We must learn new ways to live together.

We can think of our lives as circuitry, our bodies as conduits, and our minds as receptors as we rewrite the software of our existence together on planet Earth. By opening ourselves to ongoing reflection, ongoing questioning of how to contribute to healthy growth, and by taking courageous actions in place of fear and instinctive reactions, we can build new bridges. By building new bridges, we can keep ourselves from falling into the same hole. As Isaac Stern, a world famous violinist, said, *"If we don't start somehow learning to live together.... then we're doomed."*

CHAPTER THREE
STARTING WITH
THE BASICS

Using Air for Attention, Fire for Vigilance, Water for Reflection, and Earth for Discernment, a foundation is established for understanding our spiritual journey.

For our journey to have meaning, we must start with the basic personality. We must come to know ourselves and to appreciate our gifts by using our personalities to grow into the wisdom of the higher levels of awareness. An understanding of our natural differences along with the need for satisfactory group living creates tension in life. When dealing with people who have differences in their preferred expression, understanding ourselves and understanding others can assist us in maintaining objectivity. It is important to remember that individuals' personal preferences are not right or wrong, good or bad; they are only different. Each personal preference has strengths and blindspots.

There are three main types of awareness: physical, social, and imaginative or mental awareness. *"Our physical awareness is composed of our gross sense perceptions of hearing, seeing, touching, smelling, and tasting. Our emotions are more subtle, inner parts of our being and assist us in connecting to others, hence our social side. Our minds reflect yet another state of consciousness, where we can receive intuitive information, and project it through inner voices, visual images, or extrasensory perceptions. Our minds can also analytically and logically organize our knowledge and experiences."[3]*

The personality framework used in this book looks at these three awarenesses combining them into four personality profiles or expressions. Developing all three awarenesses through a dynamic interplay of the four expressions interpreted as elements can form a whole system. We can visualize this system as a triangle consisting of:

1 - AIR - OUR ATTENTION - The Mental side -
Thinking - THE DREAMER is conceptual. Taking an objective focus, the mental side provides us with an overview and a general structure of our expectations and ideas.

2 - FIRE & WATER - OUR VIGILANCE AND OUR REFLECTION - The Social side - Actions and Reactions - THE REALIST and THE CATALYST are Relational. Personally connecting to the ideas or reactions of others, the social side strives to co-ordinate, communicate, and co-operate.

3 - EARTH - OUR DISCERNMENT - The Physical Side - Doing - THE CRITIC is practical. Striving to build, make, and produce our ideas, the physical side is aware of the finiteness of limited resources, is detailed-oriented, methodical, and sensate based.

---

[3] Source: The Acupressure Stress Management Book, Acu-Yoga by Michael Reed Gach. Published by Japan Publications, Tokyo, 1981

EACH SIDE IS EQUALLY IMPORTANT

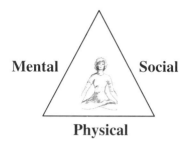

Mental   **Social**

Physical

Although we all think (mental side), feel (social side), and do (physical side), we use the sides of our awarenesses in different proportions, preferring one side to the others. We strive to use our preferred awareness as often as we can. By doing this, we more fully develop this side of our awareness thereby making it easily accessible to us. Because we favor one side of our system, we can take it for granted, as it is well developed and easy for us. As each side of our system is equally important, when these three sides of our awareness are dynamically and systematically developed and in harmony with each other, our total being expresses itself at higher levels.

UNDERSTANDING OUR PERSONAL
SOUL PSYCHOLOGY

When consciously using our natural gifts while developing those parts of us that are not so developed, we become clearer about our personal soul's mission and how to bring our personal mission forward. Our personal soul's mission is what we, in our innermost core, desire to express. This underlying soul-urge affects our decision-making processes and shapes our actions. This is the life of the Yogi, which consists of living our own divine expression and attaining self-realization.

To use this information in a practical way for developing an awareness of our personal soul psychology, we need to understand how the elements influence patterns of life's expression. The following framework is a guide to the expressions of the elements and how they affect our pursuit of holism. To identify your personal soul psychology, first review the framework quickly to obtain an overview. Then reread it and identify which of the four profiles best fits your way of expressing yourself. Keep in mind that each of us has within us all four elements and that all descriptions of these elements most likely have meant something to us at some time in our lives. Your patterns should show some general trend in how you express yourself both when balanced and unbalanced. The description that you choose should feel at least 70% a natural preference for you. For example, I have consistently expressed the pattern of Water with a second level of interest in Earth more than I have in Fire or Air. This knowledge helps me to see my strengths and my areas for growth. In my case, I am comfortable connecting to others, feeling sensitive to their needs, feeling their emotions in my own body (Water). I also want to contribute by building something tangible that has meaning to others in the world (Earth). Often, I can have trouble standing up against strong expressions of energy and may feel more inclined to back down (lacking comfort with Fire). I also have a difficult time pulling out of subjectivity as I personally relate to everyone around me (Water). I can take things too personally finding it difficult to be objective and detached (lacking comfort with Air). The capabilities for me to develop would be objectivity (Air) and expressing my own will (Fire) in order to strengthen and more easily access the complete use of my mind-body resources in my pursuit of holism. Assertiveness training would be useful in order to strengthen my own Fire or will as well as gain more objectivity of my actions and interactions with others.

If you have difficulty in recognizing your patterns and preferences, the following four chapters provide personality profiles and example struggle stories describing the expressions and struggles of each element. Reading the profiles and struggle stories may assist you in gaining clarity of your preferred personal soul psychological style of expression. After reading the next four chapters, review the framework again and choose the predominate element that best describes your more natural preference. To assist you in gaining more clarity of your preferences, each elemental chapter has:

- A personality profile describing the elemental expression
- additional information for personal development
- an example elemental 'struggle' story
- path markers clarifying the struggle's lesson
- mental exercises for increasing awareness
- physical postures or exercises for strengthening the metaphysical aspect of the element
- a worksheet for capturing cognitive insights.

PERSONAL SOUL PSYCHOLOGY FRAMEWORK USING THE ELEMENTS FOR SELF AWARENESS AND GROWTH

THE ELEMENT THE CHAKRA	AWARENESS FUNCTION	MOVEMENT TENSE	ARCHETYPE	BALANCED UNBALANCED
IDEAS **AIR** --The Air element is the aspect of our thinking mind that draws on the infinite source from above – the overmind or superconsciousness. *The gift: Attention The Chakra: Anahata*	**MENTAL AWARENESS** The AIR element represents the INTELLECT. It provides sight and overview. Its higher purpose is insight and it functions in us as a Dreamer seeing the world from a clear perspective.	**UPWARD MOVEMENT** The movement of this energy is upward and spacious. The Dreamer is oriented to the future or interplanetary time rather than Earth time.	**THE FATHER** The Air element represents the archetype of the Father, the initiator of ideas, the creator of new inventions, new concepts.	When balanced, the attention of the mature Dreamer provides us with our sense of identity and gives us focus, clarity, and compassion. When unbalanced, the immature Dreamer is detached from the world, gets confused, and flits from one idea to another, appearing intolerant of others.

THE ELEMENT THE CHAKRA	AWARENESS FUNCTION	MOVEMENT TENSE	ARCHETYPE	BALANCED UNBALANCED
ACTIONS **FIRE** -- The Fire element is an aspect of the subconscious mind providing us with a link with the thinking mind and its suggestions; it sets about making ideas into realities in a progressive forward moving fashion. *The gift: Vigilance The Chakra: Svadhistana*	**SOCIAL-MENTAL AWARENESS** The FIRE element represents the WILL. It connects our Social awareness to our Mental awareness and activates ideas through actions. The higher purpose is to light the way for others and it functions in the world as a Realist by showing us what to do next.	**UPWARD MOVEMENT** The movement of this energy is outward and upward as it evaporates water through the heat of combustion. The Realist operates in present time with a strong emphasis on the immediate requirements of a situation assisting Air in bringing ideas forward in a trial and error method.	**THE WARRIOR** The Fire element represents the archetype of the Warrior. By the friction of going against conventional ways of doing things, this function only sees the challenges in front of it. Acting "as if" all ideas are achievable, the Warrior provides new ways of doing things.	When balanced, the intuition of the vigilant mature Realist illuminates the way for others to follow. When unbalanced, the immature Realist becomes self-absorbed and uses up resources without replenishing them. Not learning from the past, the Realist burns everything up in its way, feels frustrated, and frustrates others. As if suspended in mid air, the Realist fails to build down due to the many gains and losses along the way.

THE ELEMENT THE CHAKRA	AWARENESS FUNCTION	MOVEMENT TENSE	ARCHETYPE	BALANCED UNBALANCED
REACTIONS **WATER** -- The Water element, also an aspect of the subconscious mind, responds to Air and Fire causing a catalytic reaction for expansion and growth; it links us to the conscious mind in the physical or Earth element. *The gift: Reflection* *The Chakra: Manipura*	**SOCIAL-** **PHYSICAL** **AWARENESS** The WATER element represents the IMAGINATION. It provides our reactions to the ideas of the Dreamer and the actions of the Realist. It connects our Social awareness to our Physical awareness through feelings and emotions. Its higher purpose is empowerment and it functions as a Catalyst by providing a wide range of emotions.	**DOWNWARD** **MOVEMENT** The movement of this energy is outward and downward assisting Earth in becoming less solid by bringing things to the surface to be dealt with through a catalytic cause and effect process. The Catalyst has an organic sense of time, flowing through future, past, and present in a non-linear fashion.	**THE JUDGE** The Water element represents the archetype of the Judge who surfaces emotions, resolves differences and mediates the tensions of ideas, actions, and feelings, coming up with new ways to process information and things.	When balanced, the reflection of feelings of the mature Catalyst harmonizes and blends people together by acting as our social conscience as it brings unconscious patterns for integration into the conscious mind. The immature Catalyst, when unbalanced, lacks its own form and a personal sense of self. Feelings of despair are experienced along with a murky sense of integrity.

THE ELEMENT THE CHAKRA	AWARENESS FUNCTION	MOVEMENT TENSE	ARCHETYPE	BALANCED UNBALANCED
FORMATION **EARTH** -- The Earth element is an aspect of our conscious existence. Through a sense of order and the use of reason, awareness of the finite material world is provided. *The gift: Discernment The Chakra: Muladhara*	**PHYSICAL AWARENESS** EARTH represents the BODY and provides us with structure, form, and feedback. The higher purpose is to nurture everyone and everything and it functions as a Critic by telling us what is missing.	**DOWNWARD MOVEMENT** The movement of the energy of Earth is downward as it solidifies ideas into something tangible by drawing on the wisdom of the past. By focusing on previous experiences, the Critic sees the gaps and tries to modify our processes in order to ensure the formation and manifestation of our ideas.	**THE MOTHER** The Earth element represents the archetype of the Mother and as a receptor, holds and nurtures the ideas of the Father (Air), the actions of the Warrior (Fire), and the reactions of the Judge (Water).	When balanced, the wisdom of the mature Critic acts as a stabilizing force for ensuring responsible wealth and security are manifested. When unbalanced, the immature Critic, due to feeling isolated and unappreciated, causes chaos through destructive patterns that destabilize us.

CHAPTER FOUR
Elemental Psychology
THE AIR ELEMENT
PATHMARKER #1 "ATTENTION"
Using the understanding of Air for Attention, we begin to design our life. Life is a work of art, designed by the one who lives it. Our spiritual journey begins by recognizing on what your attention is placed.

 YOUR IDENTITY AND WHERE YOUR ATTENTION LIES

HOW TO BEGIN YOUR SPIRITUAL JOURNEY

To become more conscious of your evolutionary growth and to begin your spiritual journey requires that you begin with the three awarenesses within you and your personal soul preferences for expressing itself. This beginning step in the spiritual journey will help you to establish your place on the planet (physical), your connections with others (social), and your thoughts about who you are (mental). When you can transform these awarenesses into thinking beyond me versus you, then you begin to move into the higher expressions of consciousness, developing a spiritual conscience through your finer intellect. Here you maturely and responsibly use your gifts for the benefit of everyone and everything.

Yoga psychology states that the fourth of the seven Chakras is a main seat of consciousness and resides at the heart center. The heart center provides the link between the three lower Chakras and the three upper Chakras. Here the pulsation of blood and currents of energy vibrate to all parts of your body. It is your center for perceiving the pulsation of Universal Consciousness. The Air element deals with ideas and is the aspect of our thinking mind that draws on the infinite source from above. With our attention on our future dreams and possibilities, our mental awareness is the initiator of new inventions and concepts. Here our sense of identity takes shape providing us with focus, clarity and compassion.

THE PURPOSE OF THE AIR ELEMENT

Energy expression from the fourth Chakra deals with 'who' you think you are, the purpose of your life, your identity, and the dreams you desire to fulfill.

Anahata -- The Heart Chakra
The Element of Air

 The fourth Chakra called the Anahata Chakra is associated with the heart and stimulates within the individual a desire to live a transformed life. Purity is what is desired. When the mature Air element through the Heart Chakra softens the dualistic tendencies of the first three lower Chakras, enlivened within us is the expression of compassion. *"By powerful autosuggestion govern your mind, but do not let yourself*

be governed by your material mind.[4]*"* By serving higher principles or expanded views of awareness, we ask, *"what is the best answer for this situation at this time, not what is best for me?"* In this way, we take the personal ego out of our actions. Enlivening our spirit requires that we take responsibility for our expressions.

In the Heart Chakra, we allow positive energies to transform the energies of dualism as we begin to incarnate more of the soul into our physical form through developing forgiveness, humility, and compassion. Where we would have the impulse to take flight or fight with someone about our differences, we now strive to understand and work maturely to resolve those differences.

HOW TO FULFILL AIR'S PURPOSE

The Air element needs to integrate its ideas with people in order to fulfill its purpose completely. I have seen people who are predominately developed in one awareness but exhibit little development in the other awarenesses; they are less interesting and adaptable people. Take, for example, a research scientist who wants only to sit in his or her cubicle developing new and brilliant theories. Yet, socially undeveloped, the theoretician is inept at communication and coordination. The theoretician is happy creating new ways of thinking about things but no one feels that he or she is approachable. Consequently, the scientist is left alone. On the other hand, the theoretician cannot understand what it is that people really want. Their awareness is not

---

[4] Ramamurti S. Mishra, M.D., Fundamentals of Yoga, Lancer Books, Inc. New York, 1969, p. 58-59.

adequately developed around the social elements of Fire and Water for interfacing Air with the Earth element in order to manifest their own ideas in the physical world. Not that interested in real world manifestations, they stay in their mental awareness, preferring to develop more new creative ideas. Until the theoretician can find value in developing and accessing the other elements and aspects of themselves, they will continue to gloss over the social and physical sides of their awarenesses. By believing that these sides are not that important, they often see these sides as a waste of their time. The connections, however, are often not made and ideas unfortunately can be lost.

Through self-analysis and self-awareness, you become aware of your body as a divine instrument for removing the illusion of separateness covering the Self. If you do not stay aware through self-analysis and self-awareness, then through the forces of nature you will be presented with the same opportunities for growth. In reality, without the social and physical awarenesses becoming more developed, the theoretician is cut off at the head and is out of touch with emotions and physical reactions in the body. In the process of living our lives, we try to use our natural gifts, but if we only develop our natural preference at the expense of the other three elements, we will have failed to integrate our whole system. If we choose not to grow, then we have lost an opportunity to develop and reach our full potential while we are on this Earth. The purpose of life is to know ourselves, to expand our consciousness, to share our gifts, to develop our full potential, and to bring, as Maharishi Mahesh Yogi, founder of Transcendental Meditation said, *"heaven on earth."*

THE AIR PROFILE

This profile relates to that part of us that we refer to as the intellect. Floating as if in space and detached from the physicality of Earth, this part of us draws on the forces from above. Best described by my friend, Richard, he could never understand why people settled for things as they are. Even as a child, he was always questioning why things could not be different, better, more beautiful, more interesting, more efficient. He knew his parents and his teachers found him difficult because they never quite knew what to do with him. In his words, let him describe his story as a preferred Air expression.

"I always questioned everything and would ask, why or, why not? My mind, always actively questioning what is around me, can see things and how they fit together in so many different ways. I see things that people cannot see, I guess, because they would often look at me as if I were trying to cause them problems. But I wasn't, I was trying to show them how to expand their view. I was forever telling my mother how to dress and what would add to, or take away from her outfit. '"Just add a little something there," I'd say, or "take that bracelet off and then you'll be elegant."' I love beauty and elegance and can easily recognize it when I see it. I have a natural disdain for ugliness and squalor. I want to make people see that they could aspire to finer things in life. Why not? So, I would go about telling them what to do and what not to do in order to challenge current thinking. I could never understand why people didn't take to me as I was only trying to make a better world for all of us. Never too interested in people's emotions, I think emotions are a waste of time. When people would get upset with me, I would have to scratch my head and

wonder what was wrong with them. Over the years, I have tried to learn more about people's reactions and what makes them do the things that they do. I am still not that comfortable with their personal issues, always thinking that we should be working on creating a beautiful world for everyone to live in and not bother with the rest. I suppose some people would say that I would like to create a utopia because I have tried to improve things for other people but have often been disappointed by the results displayed by them. I know what needs to be done and I'm not afraid to tell people what I see. If they don't like it, well, what can I do? I'm trying to improve things. God knows others don't see what's needed. I'm neither afraid to pour myself into projects nor am I afraid to ruffle a few feathers in the process. But, when people get bogged down with too many problems and my ideas don't seem to be coming to fruition, I can lose interest in the ideas, preferring to move on to something a little more possible; or at least something with a little more interest to me.

Sometimes I wonder if I am really meant for this world at all. I don't seem to fit into it in a way that others seem to; they appear much more comfortable accepting things as they are. I often get strange looks from people. I used to think people looked at me this way because they respected me or envied me, but now I question that. Perhaps they don't understand me at all. Neither am I a snob, nor do I want to be different from others. It is just that I see things that they don't see. I am not that interested in most things that preoccupy most people like day-to-day mundane activities or gossiping about petty things that people do. In my mind, the world could be more efficiently run. It could be more beautiful. It could be more elegant and refined. There is no need for ugliness or squalor or for people to go hungry. People could create beauty, harmony, and peace, if they paid less attention to their personal needs and to the obstacles and problems that they get so involved in. They would have a far better chance at a life that could be more significant and contribute to future generations.

My mission on this planet is, therefore, to ensure that beauty and elegance are forever in the forefront of people's minds. We should never settle for less than near perfection and even if I have to ruffle a few feathers to cause change to happen on this planet, I am prepared to do this. In fact, I must do this, and I will do this, for that is my purpose and the price I must pay to ensure that something new comes forth at all times."

THE STRUGGLE STORIES

The first struggle story and the ones that follow the other three elements are taken from personal experiences and relate to how our unconscious patterns force us into falling into dark holes due to unawareness. Sharing these stories is designed to demonstrate how easy it is to fall into holes and how painfully difficult it can be to get out of them. This in-and-out struggle, however, is the awakening process.

DIVINE DISCONTENT OF THE AIR ELEMENT HELPS TO SHAPE OUR LIVES

Living a conscious life is like living a life of divine discontent where the journey to enlightenment is the process of life itself and the process of living our life is the journey itself, and there is no end in sight. There is an expression in Yoga, 'Neti, Neti', which simply means

"Not that, not that." As I have worked with, and interpreted the concepts that our teacher, Dr. Mishra, and other spiritual masters' teachings, there is consistency around the need to question *"Who am I?"* I know in my own pursuit of self understanding, many times I have realized that I am not that, nor am I that, nope, not that either. Working with this idea of *"not that, not that,"* we can see that we have our own unique gifts. As we try to present these gifts to others, we find ourselves in situations that cause us to question ourselves. In questioning, we see we are more than just our bodies and our minds. It is not just the structure, the body or the mind that is important, it also the process. The process is that part of us that interfaces the Air with the Earth elements. This process comes out of the social awarenesses that strive to connect the ideas through Fire and Water to Earth. In this way, we create a holistic system of developing our mental, our social, and our physical awarenesses. Although we start with the structure and overview, that is, our body and our mind, we must also be awake to the process, which is activated by Fire causing reactions by Water. This process prepares the ideas of Air to be received by Earth. With only ideas, the world would not manifest new things. With only Earth, the world would not change much. With only Fire, we would not be able to sustain anything, as everything would be consumed. With only Water, everything would be washed away or muddied. We need ideas, we need actions, we need reactions, and we need the building and manifestation of something tangible. The process of using the social elements engages us in the actions and reactions of the elemental dynamics and provides the feedback we need to build something new and which is manifested in the Earth element.

The most important thing in evolving and in sorting out problems along the way is in knowing what I am after (Air) in the first place. Knowing what I am after, the actions and reactions trigger a problem-solving process which unfolds as follows: if I did not have a physical form (Earth), I could not register and interpret my experiences (Water) and then form some basis for acting on them (Fire). In registering my reactions (Water) through my sensate body (Earth), I decide what the experience means and how I am relating to it. Am I solving my problems and moving toward my objective (Air) or am I avoiding the problem-solving process and remaining in the same place? If I am engaged in a problem-solving process, I should be noticing that the tension within my body (Earth), my emotions (Water), my focused actions (Fire) and in my thinking mind (Air) disappears. If I avoid my problems, then the tension will remain there. Sometimes the tension is stronger and sometimes weaker but it will be continuous as it looks for a resolution to the problem and a consequent release from the tension. In registering and deciding about these experiences, my life starts to take shape and certain patterns can be observed. When these patterns show up consistently over time, I have started to identify both my core psychological elements that are strong in me, as well as my least preferred elements of expression that need to be developed.

Air, that part of us that is like the Father of ideas inventing new things, can often appear too detached as it floats above the world like a cloud in rarefied air, unencumbered by the physical limitations that the rest of us experience. Sometimes appearing too aloof, Air can get too full of itself, creating opportunities for deflation and humility.

THE AIR STRUGGLE STORY

WHO AM I?

Our families, Bill and his son, and I and my two daughters joined households. We all wanted to be married and did so in 1975. Both Bill and I had come from backgrounds that were stable in terms of roles and expectations. A few people were beginning to question the school systems, the religions, the community, and the male-female role expectations at this time. We were in this group of questioning people. It was the seventies and together Bill and I tried to raise our children at a time that seemed to be between two eras. Our past era, for the most part, provided us with many years of physical stability where everything seemed to appear solid, stable, and consistent. In the stable era of our youth, everything had a place and everything tangible was built to stay in place. Socially, people had jobs that often took them from the beginning of their careers to the end and provided them with decent pensions for their trouble. Women, children, and minorities somehow had to find ways to fit into this system favoring the white Anglo-Saxon man. Women became increasingly vocal as their levels of awareness grew and they saw that they must challenge the system and demand they stop being treated as second-class citizens without any power of their own. Children became more vocal as parents raised them to question authority. Native peoples started finding their voice and reclaiming their personal rights as a nation. I was also determined to take my place in the world and to use the world and all its resources for my own personal development.

Since I had no answers anyway, the journey itself was what became important and our children came along for the ride. We had family meetings incorporating the children's thoughts and questions about major decisions that affected them. We all went to 'whole-person' workshops repeatedly hearing the message, "Take responsibility for your life and question everything." We found schools that reinforced this orientation and our children grew up in a world that had not yet been saturated by personal computers, email, faxes, and cell phones, and the worldwide web, but you could feel that change was in the air and the world seemed to be in flux. Bill and I often thought of ourselves as post-latent hippies as we explored new ways of thinking and doing things. We bought a Volkswagen camper van, and between raising our children and attending university, I eagerly took up meditation, continuing my search for self-understanding. Someone said that I took on Project Danielle. My mind was soaring. My feelings were expanding. My Dreamer part of myself was alive and well and high above planet Earth. My sense of who I was and my powerful view of myself as "master of my universe" kept me in an expanded sense of myself well above the mundane ordinary patterns of everyday life.

My friend Debbie, always a few steps ahead of us on the path, suggested that we go to a special Yoga convocation to be held just outside of my hometown. I had never been to a Yoga event before and thought this would be a good experience. On the first evening there, the Yoga group met a short distance away from the buildings and built a big bonfire. I did not know that this bonfire was really a fire ceremony. Then a funny-looking dark-skinned Indian man in an orange costume led the group in singing words that I had never heard. Rama Krishna, Rama

Krishna, Krishna, Krishna, Rama, Rama. Everybody chanted these words over and over as the fire became bigger and bigger. The funny looking man kept pouring some ingredient called ghee into the fire as the chanting continued. I was mesmerized. I joined the chanting and although I did not understand the words, it did not seem to make any difference.

After the fire burnt down, there was a long period of silence and then we departed and headed back to our cabins. I remember walking back towards the buildings and someone was talking to me. My mind was crystal clear without thoughts cluttering it. I had to force myself to pay attention to this person and I turned to her and said, "I'm sorry but I simply can't think of a thing to say." She was significant to me because if she had not been there, I would not have registered the experience of such clarity of the emptiness in my mental activity -- a profound experience for any Yoga student.

As the week progressed, I started getting into the rhythm and patterns of the Yoga camp. Hatha Yoga classes in the morning, lectures on psycho-physical-spiritual development during the day, vegetarian meals, strange sitar music and group gatherings called Satsangs at night. It was at one of these Satsangs that this little orange-robed man, referred to by many as Guruji, was in front of the room performing what he called the jet-path way to enlightenment. We all sat around in a gathering of about one hundred people facing the front where there was a table set up and Guruji had an electric vibrator. He asked for a volunteer and a man coming from the crowd was informed to lie faced down on the table while Guruji chanted and moved the vibrator up and down the man's spinal column. Guruji said to pay attention and to feel the energies, the electrical system of vibration. "Feel," he said. As he was speaking these words, I fought to keep my attention on him in front of the room but something was pulling me into what felt like sleep because all I wanted to do was to close my eyes. I resisted this sensation for quite some time until I just could not resist any longer. Closing my eyes, I began floating upward into a consciousness that seemed to be spaceless and without physical form. It was an extremely charming awareness and I began relaxing into it not caring what was happening in the front of the room. I was somewhat conscious of my physical form swaying and gyrating up and down on the floor but I was more enamored by the charm of the space my attention was experiencing. Further and further out into spacelessness I went having slight impressions of beautiful beings adorned in lovely attire. I was blissful.

The next sensation I had was that of cold water being splashed on me and I was jarred back into the awareness of my physical form. I do not know how long I was gone from the room but I sensed that Guruji was in front of me and it was he that splashed me, and I was back. I cried once I realized that I was back. These tears were not tears of sadness but tears of blissful joy from the experience I felt blessed to have had. I seemed to blend into something larger and more expansive than my limited self. I experienced softness, gentleness, caring, and was charmed into longing to remain there. That experience I was to later learn, was known as Cosmic Consciousness or an expansion of unconditional awareness explained as not being limited by the physical mind and body awareness.

Now you may think that this event of my going out into such awareness was the primary event in this story, but in fact, this event was a stepping stone for what followed. People around me seemed shocked by what had happened to me, and Guruji invited everyone to write any questions down on paper and the questions could be anonymous if so desired. The next morning Bill and I were discussing the experience from the night before and Bill questioned the purpose of Guruji's trying to get the man in the front of the room to have a jet-path journey to enlightenment when I had one naturally. We thought, "Why didn't he do something more around my experience? Why did he splash me with water?" "Why don't you question him? He did say you could do it anonymously," I suggested. "I think I will," Bill said and proceeded to formulate his question. He took time ensuring that he had the right question and since he could do it anonymously, he would be straightforward with his request for an answer. The question was delivered to one of the disciples and we went about our day feeling somewhat satisfied that Bill had taken the time to construct his question thinking that it may or may not be addressed but at least he was participating.

The evening Satsang started. Guruji was sitting up on his platform in front of the room. The room was completely filled with people taking up every inch available and the summer night was hot and humid. Bill and I sat over against the wall on Guruji's far right. We felt invisible as we sat around other people. And then it began. Guruji picked up the first question. He silently read it. He put it down. He picked it up and silently read it again. He put it down again. People were getting fidgety moving around on the floor adjusting their positions and waiting for Guruji to begin the evening talk. "This questioner has a problem with his father. This questioner is taking a position that he is the authority figure and that his father does not know anything. This questioner thinks a great deal about himself and how he thinks the world should be. This questioner has a great opinion of his own identity." The piece of paper on which the question was written would be placed once again on the table. The conversation would veer off to another topic but then Guruji would pick up the same piece of paper and continued berating the questioner. He peered around the audience and his eyes would land on Bill and pause there from time to time. Bill was squirming around moving his body first in one position and then in another. The color went from his face and he wished wholeheartedly that this evening's Satsang would hurry up and be over. I felt uncomfortable for Bill as I sat next to him wanting to pretend that I did not know him, but knowing that I had encouraged him to pose the question. After all, it was anonymous, wasn't it? Then why was Guruji always looking over this way?

The night finally ended and we all shuffled out of the hall towards our bedrooms. Bill was quiet. I was quiet. We both felt like guilty children and just wanted to put this night behind us as quickly as we could. The next morning we awakened and Bill told me he did not sleep a wink all night. In fact, he said, he had to get up throughout the night to relieve his loose bowels. We got dressed and, trying to recover our dignity, began walking down the corridor to breakfast. Bill heard some commotion behind us and turned around only to see that immediately behind us walked Guruji and his entourage. Bill left my side and walked up to Guruji. "Thank you," Bill said. Guruji responded, "I do hope you forgive me."

Another layer of the ego's onionskin peeled away as Bill was forced to peer into himself and ask, "Who am I?"

> **The Air element being light, upward moving, and detached from Earth can often be experienced by others as aloof, arrogant and not available.**

Dr. Mishra reading the note and looking in our direction. Sitting next to Dr. Mishra on top of the table is Swami Janakananda Saraswati of Stockholm.

PATH MARKER #1 -- ATTENTION

Once you are on your spiritual path, you do not know where and when your teacher will show up. Be prepared by keeping your attention on where you are going and how you are getting there. Through self-analysis, you can avoid a superior sense of yourself from taking hold of you. You are lucky to have someone attack this sense of yourself so that you can remember to be humble and grateful. Our higher self is beyond the dualistic aspect of the ego mind and its need to be important. Once enlightened, your self-identity, or ego, surrenders its control to the higher self rather than the other way around.

WHO ARE YOU?

One night I had a dream that I was waiting in a long line-up. We were all waiting to enter an inner sanctum where Dr. Mishra was sitting cross-legged on a platform. Directly in front of him, another platform existed with a screen against the back wall. We were arranged in the line-up in some pre-determined fashion that resulted in our standing in front of the screen one at a time while our lives were portrayed behind us. *"Who are you?"* was the question asked and each person would relate their life story and the lessons they struggled with while living their lives with others on this planet. *"Who am I?"* is the question posed in pursuit of self-knowledge. This is not just a simple question of "what do I do" or "whom should I marry." We must get to know the qualities our souls want to express while in our physical forms during our lifetime. Until there is this level of self-understanding and self-acceptance, we cannot wisely use the materials that are offered to us in human form. We begin our self-analysis by using our Air element for identifying our dreams and providing an overview of our ideas for serving the world. We reach up to the Dreamer in us for tapping into our intellect and creating something new. We activate our heart center, where the Dreamer resides, by striving to operate with humility, tolerance, and compassion. If we get too detached, then natural law will bring us down and force us into a more balanced approach for living.

THE GRADUAL EMERGING SELF

It is not unusual to see that when our unconscious patterns show up around an enlightened person, our learning experiences speed up and the process of confronting the tension between our intellect with its beliefs, expectations, and the real world we live in are brought to the forefront of our attention. Our emerging unconscious needs become available energy for use on the conscious level and the Self is created, Jung says, *"as a kind of compensation for the conflict between the inner and the outer worlds."* The Self is *"something that has come into being only very gradually and has become a part of our experience at the cost of great effort. Thus the Self is also the goal of life, because it is the most complete expression of that fateful combination we call 'individuality.'"*[5]

The interesting part of the spiritual journey is that we have gently to invite the ego, which is attached to the relative world of the material life, into surrendering its hold on our physical selves and join us on the journey of experiencing the non-ego or higher Self. Because the

---

5 Jung, Two Essays, p. 268.

higher Self, or soul, is unseen, asking the ego to surrender to the soul's purpose is like asking water to be the center of awareness for the fish. *What is water? Where is the water?* If the fish could understand that it is swimming in the substance that sustains itself, then it could more consciously appreciate the unseen, all pervasive water. Like the fish, our ego is asked to go along with the higher discerning Self. The higher discerning Self is already there and requires that the ego work with it in order to serve the Self rather than the ego servicing itself in a dualistic world that pits itself against everything else.

EVERYTHING IS YOUR GURU

Always grateful to have Dr. Mishra as our spiritual teacher, we first met him in 1977, two years after we were married. Meeting Guruji, otherwise known as Dr. Ramamurti Mishra, was like coming home. Over the years of being around Guruji while he was in his physical body, along with continued study of Yoga and understanding mind-body differences, we had many experiences that kept us on the path of self-analysis, self-discovery, and the pursuit of self-knowledge. These experiences continuously challenged our limited sense of our egos and ourselves. But Dr. Mishra used to say, *"You don't really need me; a dog can be your guru. If you observe the dog, it will teach you something. Everything that happens to us can teach us something,"* Guruji used to say that coming to the Ashram was like coming to a De-Mental Institution. It seemed that lessons of life often got quickly stimulated when visiting the ashram. Always some drama among people manifested and this drama usually provided great material for the evening discussion during Satsang. For our minds are too attached to our sense of ourselves and there is a great need for the teacher to assist us in releasing the ego's hold over us. Always displaying a keen sense of humor, he related a story of police officers bringing a "crazy" person to the psychiatric hospital he worked in and he would say to the officers, *"You stay, he can go."* If we get too stuck in the material world, then we can arrest the process of self-discovery.

DREAMER – AIR – ATTENTION
MENTAL AWARENESS
DEVELOPING FLOW

To develop compassion, tolerance, and humility, the metaphysical aspects of the Anahata, fourth center of awareness in the heart region, the following postures are useful. Standing straight and tall with your hands in the prayer position at the Heart Chakra, visualize the heart and see it expanding out into the world, filling the world with loving energy and intentions. Notice your breathing and see the whole universe within you. Feel that connection and expand it outward until it reaches up and even further upward into the finer energies of the universe. Tap into those finer energies by breathing them back down into mother earth using concentrated breathing as you bend forward. Feel the energy coming up from mother earth into your body through the feet, the legs, the trunk of the body, into the heart center, through the neck, up into the head, and out through your crown Chakra. Perform this flow three or four times as you breathe in coming up and out going down. Do the flow slowly and with attention. Feel an expansion of yourself; feel this electro-magnetic energy vibrating both within and around you. You are the connection. You are the vital link in the evolution of world consciousness. Bring your hands back to the heart center in the prayer position. Feel it. Experience it. Live it.

SUMMARY OF THE AIR ELEMENT FOR SPIRITUAL GROWTH

The upraised sword of attention uses our Mental abilities to cut through the illusion of false attachments and sees clearly the truths that can set us free.

When a balanced and mature expression is developed, the individual expresses intelligence, compassion, forgiveness, and humility while living a life of humanitarian service in the world.

When unbalanced and immature, the individual's life becomes self-centered, intolerant of others and deteriorates into a stern attitude resulting in an abandoned, lonely person. Creating pie-in-the sky ideas and flitting from one business enterprise to another, the creation of new ideas never quite materializes into anything useful in the world.

CAPTURING COGNITIVE INSIGHTS
WORKSHEET

To tap into our spiritual selves at the heart level, mentally ask the question, *"What can I do to enliven my spirit and create situations for myself and others to constructively evolve?"*

_____

_____

_____

_____

_____

_____

_____

_____

_____

_____

_____

_____

CHAPTER FIVE
Elemental Psychology
THE FIRE ELEMENT
PATHMARKER #2 "VIGILANCE"
Using the understanding of Fire for Vigilance, we develop our will in order to activate our Dream and test our thoughts out in the real world. How are you responding to your life?

 **YOUR PERSONAL POWER AND HOW TO USE IT**

THE PURPOSE OF THE FIRE ELEMENT

When we are dealing with third Chakra energies, we are dealing with the development of our inner strengths, our will, and our personal power. The Fire element deals with actions and is an aspect of our subconscious mind providing us with a link with our thinking mind. With vigilance, the Fire element person is action-oriented and will act for its own sake illuminating the way for others to follow. Fire burns and activates us through friction so people with Fire preferences are people who ensure that we are not bogged down with too many details or too many feelings and often agitate us to move on more quickly than we may be ready to do. Taking the ideas of the Air person, the Fire dominant person jumps into immediate action and starts to move the ideas forward through an iterative process "as if" the idea should work.

Through this trial and error process, we begin to know directly what works and what does not work in a way that wastes no time in what appears to them to be superfluous details, because Fire people often feel they do not have time to waste.

Manipura -- The Solar Plexus Chakra
The Element of Fire

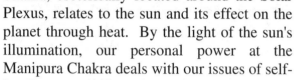

The third Chakra, esoterically located around the Solar Plexus, relates to the sun and its effect on the planet through heat. By the light of the sun's illumination, our personal power at the Manipura Chakra deals with our issues of self-esteem and self-responsibility. Here the struggle is the use of personal power in appropriate ways to generate conscious, responsible actions forcing us to take risks and to develop self-confidence through creative activities with our relationship to money, power, and position in life.

HOW TO FULFILL FIRE'S FOCUSED WILL

Vigilance, the gift of the Fire person, is also what causes pain for that person when not utilized. Vigilance used as focused energy for the benefit of humanity rather than for the selfish needs of their own unconscious instinctive drives is the mature use of this element. When, however, the focused will operates mainly from instinctive forces without the use of our more rational conscious mind, our actions can create artificial worlds that soon tumble.

THE FIRE PROFILE

The Fire profile relates to that part of us which links our subconscious mind with the intellect. My friend, Janet, best describes this element. Janet simply wants to solve problems. She thinks the most important thing to do is to move ideas forward by finding new solutions.

In her words, *"That's the way I've always been inclined and that's the way I prefer to be. Like the Air preferred person, I also see things quickly. Answers come to me just as if I am breathing them in. I don't know where they come from, they just come and I act on them. I am faced with a problem and then I can see an answer. I move on that information and take steps that cause things to happen. For me, it's not just the idea that is important but the actions to move the idea forward. I have often been in a room full of people and have never understood why people just sit there and do or say nothing. This I don't understand. Are they not interested? Are they stupid? Don't they care? I always seem to be the one who kicks into gear first. My motors are revving. "Let's get going," I would think to myself. Why all this sitting around chatting or arguing about what to do. "Here's an idea, let's just do it." Why I always have to be the one to cause things to happen, I don't know, but that's how I've always been. It's as if people like me don't have enough time in our life and we have to focus and stay in activity so we don't waste any of it. My energy appears high to others because I simply take what's in front of me and act on it. I can see immediate things that can be done and how they can come together to achieve goals. I have no problem in finding immediate answers to questions that others scratch their heads over. I don't get bogged down with past data, future day dreaming, or emotional issues, so it's easy for me to be immediate and focused. Sometimes people take offense because they think I'm overbearing or arrogant, but that is not what I'm trying to be. I simply want to get moving on things so there is no time wasted. If I am really focused, I can appear to be impatient and can get frustrated when things don't go fast enough for me. I'll go off and daydream if it gets too boring for me and my approaches aren't appreciated. If this happens in a group, I tend to shut down and want to get out of there in a hurry.*

Personally I've always been very handy and can work mechanical things easily, fix things quickly, work with tools putting things together, whatever. If there is something in front of me requiring fixing, organizing or moving, I can do it. I don't see what gives other people problems around things like that. "Just do it!" is an expression that suits people with my preference very well. One thing I have noticed about myself in the course of my life is that I sometimes don't hold on to things. I have made and lost lots of money, possessions and relationships in the past. Things tend to disappear around me from time to time. I also notice that I may not take as good care of my body as some of my colleagues do of theirs. Oh, I know that I may take on too many projects but when people ask me for my advice, I find it hard to pull away, taking such pleasure in problem solving as I do. Because of this nature, I may become overloaded from time to time and not even notice that I've done it again. Once in awhile, my body may break down as if to say, "that's enough!" I would like it if I could register this awareness a little earlier in the game so that I don't have to be ill in order to take a rest. I'm working on this. I'm also working on having more patience with other people's paces. I know that other people don't see moving on things as vitally important as I do and so I am trying to understand their process and to work more closely in alignment with them. But, you have to know that I'm like a horse at the starting gate, revving to go and by slowing my process down, my energy gets backed up in me. It is as hard for me to slow myself down as it might be for others to pick up speed to keep up with me.

My mission on this planet is to serve others by providing them with my ability to see clearly what needs to be done next and to come up with creative approaches for solving problems. As long as I'm contributing to projects and people in that way, I feel that I am using my talents and skills wisely. If there is a problem to be solved, call me."

TENSION MOVES US TOWARD OUR ACTIONS

Feeling that they have no time to waste, the fast-paced Fire person uses their energy in producing a continuous flow of output. Moving from one busy activity to another, the focused energy of the Fire preferred person gets impatient when things are not moving fast enough in their lives. They might find that they get bored with too many details, numbers, or limiting parameters, finding these too restrictive and uninteresting. They would rather just keep moving onto the next set of actions. They have to be careful that they do not build a house without a foundation, as the physical side is not being tended to and may not continue to support them. Not tending to the physical world, the fast-paced Fire person uses up everything around them in their mad pursuits. Jung says, *"Man is not a machine in the sense that he can constantly maintain the same output of work. He can only meet the demands of outer necessity in an ideal way if he is also adapted to his own inner world, that is to say, if he is in harmony with himself."[6]*

THE FOCUSED ENERGY OF THE FIRE PERSON

When we are not in harmony with our total system, those areas of growth that we need for balance are often the areas we find most boring and want to gloss over. Feeling important because we are so busy, we lose sight of 'quality of life' issues and eventually, the body, the relationships, or the physical world we live in, breaks down. As if running on steam and driven by some unconscious force, the focused energy of the Fire dominant person revs up the human instrument and focuses its energy on some goal. In the *Philosophy of the Unconscious* by Eduard von Hartmann, the will, he says, has an inner purpose which is not conscious and which drives all the life forces in the direction of its aims. These drives, if not stopped and analyzed, will continue to exert pressure in the human personality beyond the controls of the rational conscious mind.

THE WAVE OF ARROGANCE AND
THE WAVE OF IGNORANCE

Two mental waves can capture the immature Fire expression if not watched and observed vigilantly. The first wave is that of arrogance as the mind harbors thoughts that it can do anything. By obtaining success, the arrogant Fire person feels conceited and these feelings of conceit bring hypocrisy. Full of their own

[6] C. G. Jung, *Contributions to Analytical Psychology*, trans. By H. G. and C. F. Baynes

importance, they continue to be driven by their own force without regard for others. Using resources up as soon as, or even before, they have them, the Fire person causes frustrations for those around them as others begin to feel used and abused.

The second mental wave to be aware of when the immature Fire energy takes hold of the mind is that of ignorance. Acting like a child, the unbalanced Fire expression learns nothing from its experiences and continues to live mainly in the present. Seeing everything as if it should be available for them, the child-like immature Fire wants to consume everything. With little judgement and understanding of right or wrong, this childlike pattern grasps everything for consumption with little regard for the environment or for others. Operating from this level of ignorance, the immature Fire is returned back to the starting gate empty-handed once again having exchanged short-term comfort for long-term pain.

When the aims of the unchecked Fire element, however, take hold of our actions completely, time and space are involved and these real parameters and limitations are felt as tension in the body and mind when moving too rapidly towards fixed points. When, however, we are operating from a more balanced expression of the focused will, we can rely on the direct results of our actions.

THE FIRE STRUGGLE STORY

WHO DID I THINK I WAS?

I was determined to develop my will as I always felt that I was not strong enough for the real world. A nurturer by nature, I take care of other people's needs first and my needs may not be addressed. So I purposely set out to become stronger in my expressions and I thought I would do this by being committed to my career. Being driven by my will, I felt I had no time to waste as I was almost forty and felt I had a lot of catching up to do. My first job was 'cold calling' organizations for head hunting and placing people into engineering or accounting positions. Downtown Bay Street Toronto after years of meditative yoga camps was intense. The president of the company I worked for would sit at meetings and with a fist made with one hand, he would punch it into the palm of the other hand while leaning forward in his chair anxiously ready to receive any new data. We would work at our desks until 10:00 and would quickly get up, grab our paper and pencils, and rush into a glass-enclosed office where we would report on our activities. I had to keep good notes or I would not have much to say which, of course, would be defeating the whole purpose of being there. Talk fast, walk fast, think fast, do fast. That was the pace and you had to keep pace. I kept this up for a short time but found that it was too intense for me. I did, however, learn how to stay on the telephone. I had been told that if you want to have a career as a female and be taken seriously, you had to be in sales. Being in sales meant you had to become comfortable with cold calling.

My next position was coordinating seminars in a top-of-the-line management development organization. I thought I had died and gone to heaven, for here was a direct route for personal and professional growth, and I gobbled it up. This was another fast-paced environment where people asked you if you had a part-time job when you left work before 5:30 or 6:00 p.m. having arrived before 8:00 or 8:30 and more likely than not, worked through your lunch hour. Heaven forbid that you had a personal life outside of this place. Here I got to see some of the top-notch speakers of the world and it proved invaluable. Invaluable because I could see that these speakers did not agree on where we were all going and what the best approach to getting there was.

From there, I took a position with a female medical doctor who wanted to sell stress management and other training and development workshops and services to businesses combined with a beauty parlor cum health spa. Again, I thought I had died and gone to heaven. Here I could use so much of my training. For example, my yoga training and natural healing arts backgrounds were used as stress management tools. My degree in psychology and human resources development was used to develop human potential development and health-related workshops. My ability to stay on the telephone helped me in selling and coordinating training and development events. In this position, I had the opportunity to organize and start-up an enterprise, set up books, create operation processes, and make all the connections necessary to run a full line of health and management services with the human resources required to do it. I started up the educational department, hired and fired people, and without investing any of my own money, learned to run a business. On top of that, I was beginning to make a decent salary. This part of my career took place in the most elite part of town and the educational-beauty parlor-health spa was a concept I liked very much. The position and the intelligent spa concept was, however, ahead of its time, coming at the peak of the financial boom but just before the financial bust.

My next position was selling and delivering management development training with a small family-owned firm teaching a system for understanding behaviour and how to work with people's differences. My salary increased as well as my sense of my own importance. Around this time, a girlfriend who had been coaching me throughout this career development process, told Bill and me of her interest in speculating in the condominium complex we were planning to move to once we sold our home. She was a person who was after power, position, and wealth. And, she was a strong dominant Fire person. I was a person originally on a spiritual journey wanting to serve self and others through the development of self-awareness principles. However, I was caught up in the fire and desire for power, position, and wealth. When and how this happened I can't say, but it did and I was on a fast track earning more money in a shorter period of time than my husband who had worked many years to achieve his income level.

Now, years ago, just before my first husband David died, we had moved into a house at 22 South Elm Street in our hometown. Shortly after the move, a flood hit our hometown and everything and everyone went into aftermath shock. Seven months after the flood, David had died in an automobile accident. Moving into 22 South Elm Street was the beginning of our disaster as a family and a couple. After his death, I swore I would never live in a number 22 again because of the drastic changes in my life right after our move. This is where I was when the flood hit, this is where I lived when my husband died, and this is where I lived when I lost my religion, my city, my country and all the support structures that had given me security. Never again.

But my girlfriend, whose path was different in its expression from my own, but whose influence was affecting how I saw myself, came to us and proposed a partnership to speculate making some good money quickly. We were in the process of selling our home as the children had moved out and, after all, I was a very busy executive. We were considering moving into one of the condominium buildings when my friend approached us with this offer. Neither Bill nor I had any major resistance to the idea, nor did we jump at the chance, after all, we did not see ourselves as risk takers really. But having more money was enticing and strangely enough neither Bill nor I spoke about it too much. Bill thought that I wanted to speculate and I thought that was what he wanted. Our friend thought that we both wanted to speculate and went ahead and made offers on two more condominiums.

We did sell our house and moved into a condominium, but due to the availability of units at the time we moved, when we were ready to close on our home, the only available condominium was in the building numbered 22 rather than the one I originally wanted in building 20. Not only was the universe trying to tell me to pay attention by the number, but also the new address was 22 South Port Street instead of 22 South Elm Street. I did not pay attention. Now I should have known better because I was on a spiritual path and I could see these things coming, couldn't I? "Maybe this time it's different. Maybe this time, 22 won't be so hard on me," I thought. "How bad could it be? Real estate sales were growing rapidly and the worst case scenario may be that we don't make as much money as we originally thought." This is what my mind said. Before the ink dried on our mortgage deals, however, the real estate market took a nose-dive. The ton of money we had made on selling our house was soon diminishing as we watched our condominium investment depreciate minute by minute before our eyes. I was frightened because this was our home and our security and I lacked the faith that things would turn out all right. I started having physical symptoms. Interestingly enough I was bleeding profusely from the womb which symbolically represented my feelings of blame and shame of losing our home, our own inner sanctum -- our womb, as every day the situation seemed to become worse.

Our friend, having the strong element of Fire, tried her best to take care of us but in a way that made us uncomfortable. For example, our real estate agent told us it would be better to sell quickly and get out of the situation. Our friend, however, called the agent's manager and said to keep that agent away from us, as she was depressing. Now Bill and I did not know that this had happened until I realized we had not heard from our agent for awhile and I called her. She seemed surprised that I did not know her manager had been called and that she was informed by her manager to stay away from us.

A greater sense of fear set in when we realized that we had given up control of our own financial lives for gaining more money. What happened to our path? How did we get off it? How did this happen? Having moved so quickly along my career path, I felt I could do just about anything and do it quickly. I went from feeling dependent on others, to feeling independent of others. I simply got too greedy, too big for my breeches and, ultimately was slapped down. After all, "Who did I think I was?"

The Fire element, being hot and light, strives to heat things up in its attempt to create focused actions. However, people can be turned off as these actions are often interpreted as dominating, arrogant, and insensitive to the needs of others. The Fire element is outward and upward moving. Fire invents new ways of doing things as intuitive flashes trigger spontaneously actions.

Dr. Mishra and the Fire Ceremony

PATH MARKER #2 - VIGILANCE

Be always vigilant on your path. Do not get too clever. If there is an untruth somewhere, or if you have lost the main purpose of your soul's journey, the truth has to be brought out into the light in order to set you back on your true path again. Be grateful for the lesson. Take responsibility for the results in your life and stop looking to blame others.

WHO DID I THINK I WAS?

In the story, "WHO DID I THINK I WAS," I became too full of my own personal power and lost my spiritual focus. The energy in the Solar Plexus Chakra had to be corrected. When people become too full of themselves, situations in life begin to create opportunities that force us to topple. When we are thrown overboard through a chaotic event, we draw back into ourselves and are forced to re-examine our lives.

SELFLESS SERVICE

To tap into our spiritual selves at the Solar Plexus level, selfless service and listening skills become more important than selfish enterprises and giving others our answers for all their problems. When providing people with answers to their problems, remember that every person must be responsible for their own actions in order to learn and achieve balance in their lives. Once balanced, using listening and gentle guidance, the plane of illumination becomes evident and the higher expressions of the Solar Plexus Chakra are realized. Yoga teaches us that a restless impulsive mind cannot concentrate. Dr. Mishra says, *"Truth in speech, simplicity in manner, and firmness of mind are infallible Divine instruments to certain success."*[7]

The Fire element, in order to express its spiritual aspect, strives to open its mind to a more conscious, rational, and sensitive approach for service to humankind. There are times when the force of the Fire element is necessary to stir things up. However, there are also times when people require a "softer" approach. It is the struggle of the Fire element person to see and feel which approach is best for the other people involved. For tapping into spiritual expressions, we can ask, *"What is my purpose and what are the consequences of my actions on others?"* In this way, we build in a rational approach by analyzing rather than letting our instincts run our activities in life. This is intelligent intuition where the intuition provides answers, but before actions are incorporated, benefits and consequences are reviewed.

---

[7] Ramamurti S. Mishra, M.D., Fundamentals of Yoga, Lancer Books, Inc., New York, 1969, p. 56.

WARRIOR – FIRE – VIGILANCE – WILL
AWARENESS DEVELOPING FLOW

To develop vigilance, proper use of intuition, and the intelligent, rational use of a strong, forceful will, which are the metaphysical, higher aspects of the Solar Plexus or Manipura, third center of awareness, the following postures are useful. The Warrior pose assists in the coordination of the body with the mind by use of focused tension throughout the posture flow. Stand with arms out at shoulder height. Spread the feet three or four feet apart and bend the left knee. Shift the body toward the left, looking at your left hand as you move in this direction. Hold the pose and concentrate on the mighty energy of the warrior. Feel the tension in the legs, arms, and shoulders as your is focused on truth, being and light. Be vigilant, concentrate, focus and breathe. Now bring the palms of your  hands together lifting them up toward the heavens. Look up. Hold the pose for a few seconds. Breathe. Repeat on the opposite side of the body by bending the right knee and looking up toward the folded hands. Follow the Warrior's pose with the Corpse pose. Become aware of the body 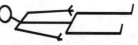 in its resting state. Become conscious of the body's contact points with the floor. Surrender into the floor, letting the body melt into a silent state of deep relaxation. When the Warrior learns to follow each activity with a deep rest, they learn to balance their energy flow, to maintain inner harmony, and to use their energy in powerful ways for service to the world. Maharishi Mahesh Yogi says, *"Rest is the basis of activity."*

SUMMARY OF THE FIRE ELEMENT FOR SPIRITUAL GROWTH

 The dynamic and fiery energy of intuition falls as leaves from the tree dropping sparks of inspiration and creativity. Using vigilance, the ever-ready warrior is action oriented, enlisting the aid of others in bringing ideas out of the realm of concepts.

When balanced, mental strength is used to dispense original approaches to all problems. Insights come as easily as breathing in air. Leading others is conveyed through expressive vitality. Trusting the flow of intuition, the focused, fiery energy is used in a conscious approach for illuminating the world and thereby achieving spiritual success.

When unbalanced and immature, a life of conflict and loss is evidenced. The job never gets done. People turn away because of frustrations and differences of opinions. The instinctive need for irrational, constant change makes for headstrong and impulsive actions and differences of opinion are quickly turned into quarrels.

CAPTURING COGNITIVE INSIGHTS
WORKSHEET

For tapping into spiritual expressions, we can ask, *"What is my purpose in this situation and what are the consequences of my actions on others?"*

_____

_____

_____

_____

_____

_____

_____

_____

_____

_____

_____

CHAPTER SIX
Elemental Psychology
THE WATER ELEMENT
PATHMARKER #3 "REFLECTION"
Using the understanding of Water for Reflection, we develop our emotions as the world and others in it create tension which forces us to reflect, recreate, reconstruct ourselves as we blend in with others. How are you feeling about your life?

YOUR IMAGINATION, REFLECTION, AND HOW TO TAP INTO IT

THE PURPOSE OF THE WATER ELEMENT

The Water element deals with our reactions to the ideas of the Air and the actions of the Fire elements. These reactions stimulate a catalytic response for expansion and growth by linking the mind to the physical element of Earth. Through our reactions, our emotions are reflected upon and our imagination is stimulated. When we are dealing with second Chakra energies, we are dealing with the development of our imagination and how to honor our feelings by learning how to appropriately express them. We strive to build intimate, mature relationships with others by sharing our feelings, harmonizing, blending, and integrating with others through affiliation and cooperation.

The Water element in us, or the re-creation part of ourselves, assists in shaping and reshaping our "material" selves. We do this by asking, *"where are we, who are we with, what are we trying to do, how are we doing it, and how are we feeling in this situation?"* In each situation, we are mixing our own reactions, understanding, and connections with what is happening around us. In this way, we transform ourselves to the degree of our conscious connections to the data that is stimulating us. We alter or recreate the situation out of our recognition and reflection of the situation.

Svadhisthana -- The Reproductive Chakra
The Element of Water

 The second Chakra, which is related to the moon and the effects of the moon on water, is esoterically located around the reproductive organs. Fluctuations of water on Earth during phases of the moon stir our emotions making us sensitive to the physical Earth (the body) and how we are personally relating to our place on Earth. Svadhishthana encompasses fertility and procreation as we strive to make physical connections with family, friends, and society. Our struggle at the second Chakra is to consciously experience physical feelings. These sensations of feelings cause us to reflect about our lives. This reflection can stir our imagination and our fantasies. Once stimulated, we long to re-create, re-produce and re-enact the worlds of possibilities in life through creative processes.

HOW TO FULFILL THE NEED FOR THE WATER ELEMENT

Our soul's purpose is incarnating higher expressions into the body of matter by use of the four elements found in the individual personality. By tapping into and developing these elements, the soul requires that the individual develop its conscious *knowing of itself.* The Water element brings this process to a more personal experience through our interpretations of our feelings. The Water element acts as a catalyst for the other elements ensuring that the proper use of the expressions is sensitive to the whole expression of the four elements. Without a well-developed Water element, the other elements are not as realized as they could be. The registration of our feelings is a vital and catalytic basis of information. Assisting in the spiritual growth and development process, Water mediates the tensions triggered by the ideas of Air, the actions of Fire, and prepares the way for the integration of both Air and Fire with the Earth element. When, for example, we have feelings of anger coming from our Fire element, we can act constructively by letting people know what is happening with us. We do not attack, but we share the basis for these feelings with them. In this way, we are providing feedback as a participant in life and perhaps assisting others in seeing that they are overstepping some boundaries. When we are depressed, our sensate bodies are telling us to express ourselves, to stand up for ourselves, to bring out the Warrior in us represented by our Fire element that we are failing to use because our Water element is damping our will. When we are confused about "who" we are, or when we have too grand a picture of our own importance, our sensate body feels stressed as the mind strives to clarify what is actually happening. The mind would not bother to clarify if the feelings of confusion were not present. The reactions triggered by the feelings help to surface differences for mediating the tension of the ideas and the actions. This mediation assists in the manifestation of results by being an interface for processing data and preparing the way for the physical distinctions of Earth. In many ways, the Water element acts as our social judge in life assisting us in dealing with issues that affect us. Everything tangible comes through awareness of sensations of feelings in the body -- this is nature's gift to us. This is our feedback machine. We cannot change unless we get, give, and work with, this important data. With feedback from both the internal and the external worlds comes increased awareness of the whole system. With increased awareness, we become more conscious.

"Knowing ourselves" is developed through life experiences and analysis. If we do not learn things on our own and open up to what life is presenting to us, then life will repeatedly present us with opportunities to grow. Our lessons will come to us in one way or another, but until we comprehend the lesson, we will be presented with continual opportunities for growth.

THE WATER PROFILE

The Water element links the subconscious mind with the conscious mind and is described by me, a predominately Water element person with a strong connection to the element of Earth.

"As a child, I was naturally drawn to mediate problems in the family, being able to understand all sides of an issue. I wanted to ensure that everyone felt heard and that they worked toward some mutually satisfying resolution. Not taking a clear stand on anything except that people should get along with each other, I lacked a strong identity of my own and seemed to go pleasantly along with the flow of things. Taking this "flow of things" approach, I appeared to be lacking in form as Water tends to take on the shape of its current environment, context, or container. People probably didn't know me very well because I would show one shape of myself to this person and another shape to that person. After reading a novel, I would take on the characteristics of the heroine. I spoke up for the causes of others often putting their needs above my own. I didn't feel that my needs were that important because my needs would keep changing, as I was never quite sure what my current needs were. As I matured and started learning from my actions and behaviors, I eventually registered feedback from that side of my personality that relates more to the Earth element. I began to see that by taking this action, I would get certain feedback from others that would nurture me and make me happy. If I took a different set of actions, those actions would jar me by the reactions I would get from others and this would make me unhappy.

Being predominately Water, it was not unusual for me to pick up the feelings of those around me. Sometimes I wasn't sure if the feelings I had were my own or if they actually belonged to someone else. I was like a sponge and absorbed feelings into me – water and earth can make for murky water. Having a strong sense of social justice and especially sensitive to the underdog, I was quick to pick up the slightest word, gesture, or feeling that could hurt someone. I then had to make things better for that person. After the death of my first husband, my Fire element came in full force and for the first time in my life, I started demanding things for myself. Because I was new to Fire in my late twenties, Fire was expressed in an immature fashion. I rudely offended people that I loved in ways that I would never do today without serious regrets. Once I got used to the Fire burning in me, I had to learn to temper it so that it wouldn't come up in unexpected ways and throw me off guard. I needed to be able to draw on its use but I also wanted to have choice around using the force of my own will. Being sensitive to others, I knew that I would have to pay the price of guilt for using this force unconsciously since Fire is not my preferred element.

My least developed element is that of Air, which could provide me with the objectivity I need in order to stop personalizing the world around me. Over the years, I have learned to go up to the mountaintop in the form of meditation in order to develop my Air element. Although I love the mountaintop and meditation, I also know deep inside of me that I cannot stay there very long, as my calling is connecting with people and their feelings. That is where I belong and that is how I can best use my gifts and talents. I know, however, from experience that I must go to the mountaintop to empty my sponge from all the emotions it has absorbed as well as to remind myself that everything looks better from a broader perspective. My activity, however, belongs on the Earth's plane connecting with others and using my Personal Soul Psychology in a way that helps empower self and others. This I have only learned through diligent work on myself along with accepting myself and including myself in the formula of caring for people in the world. I strive hard not to take on the ways of others, but to learn how I can be true to myself. Because I have Earth in me, whatever I do must have practical applications.

I like to mix the world of the Earth (the body) and all its humanness with the flow of the Water (feelings), the force of the Fire (focused attention), and the objectivity of Air (ideas) for developing all aspects of my human potential. In doing this, I am naturally fulfilling my life's mission. This is how I would describe my work: fulfilling my spiritual mission on the planet."

WE CANNOT BECOME TOTALLY UNAWARE AGAIN

Once our spiritual journey begins, it is not possible to hide behind the filters that prevent us from seeing clearly. Ignorance has been lifted and we have no choice but to take our place in life and be responsible for our results. We might have periods when we fool ourselves or there might be times when we feel we are not evolving; but once we have looked through the filters that are preventing us from seeing clearly, we can not pretend to hide behind them again. If we do pretend, we also know that there are consequences to pay.

ACCEPTANCE OF OURSELVES

There is nothing in life so painful as not accepting the natural gifts we have to offer others. When we do not accept ourselves, we often fail to contribute the gifts that are unique to us. Acceptance comes from our own awareness of our natural gifts. Once we see and know what these gifts are then we can develop them. In working to raise our awareness, we have to begin by charming or gently encouraging the individual personal ego into becoming the servant of the soul or Universal Divine energy. As the individual ego is gently encouraged to participate in this work, then the soul's own intelligence can shine through the vehicles or human instruments called you and me. When your personal soul psychology is maturely expressed, the soul shines brightly through transmitting the finer qualities of discernment, vigilance, compassion, tolerance, intelligent intuition, reflection, and responsibility. These finer qualities enliven, integrate, and holistically expand, as opposed to segregate and diminish the human family. We pursue our holistic approach by moving beyond the dualistic pulls of either you win or I win, which are ego-based, into focusing our attention on service and community. To gently encourage the individual ego into higher Self-expressions, we do not tell the ego what to do, as this will only cause the ego to dig its heels in more deeply and find reasons for not cooperating. Egos are good for these types of thought forms. We rather invite the ego through open-ended questions, such as *"What is the best solution for everyone in this situation and how best can I assist with what I know and do best?"* In this way, the ego-self can comfortably begin serving the higher Self by using its own gifts and capacities for service to humanity -- this should be something the ego would naturally like to do.

THE NEED FOR REFLECTION

Reflection is a secondary activity not based on primary actions in the present tense. As the moon's light is from the sun, our reflections come from the activities and the people who are involved in our lives. We reflect on these activities and how we are being treated in the world around us. This reflection triggers within us a process of deciding how we want to be or not be when dealing with others. We might start by daydreaming possibilities of "if only" I did this or "if only" I did that. This daydreaming causes us to create and generate fantasies and imagination. When Water-element people feel unsafe in their world, they tend to hold back, thinking people will laugh at them. In holding back their natural tendencies to play with the world's materials, they fail to generate feedback within themselves of just how creative and imaginative their processes can be. When our fears prevent us from fantasizing, we get bored, flat, and take a non-participatory position in life where we participate in the world but not with the world. As a result of this position, creativity and imagination do not get activated within us. The Water in us relates to procreation through fantasy and imagination, which can be used to advantage in the creative arts such as writing, acting, or story telling, as examples. When we are dull inside, little excites us and our enthusiasm for life is diminished as passion is lacking. If we are lucky, life will present us with a major crisis that either wakes us up to the importance of taking risks as opposed to sending us further within ourselves. Hopefully, most Water-element people get awaken and take risks.

THE WATER STRUGGLE STORY

I BECAME A SEEKER

In June of 1972, my hometown experienced a flood and most of the town's people were under the strain of recovery from the devastation. We learned that the flood was not the problem. The recovery and the psychological loss of personal and sentimental items such as photos were the problem. Losses such as these made people unhappy and confused about their lives. Recorded memories ensured them of their place in the scheme of things. My husband, David, and I also felt the strain of the flood's devastation in our lives. Our strain took the form of an emotional split in our relationship after housing many flood-victim people for five months. I made the mistake of offending my sister-in-law by requesting that her children, who were close to my own age, do more chores around the house. I had never knowingly offended anyone who reacted so strongly before and was taken by surprise when she took such offense to this request by leaving our house for good. I felt shut out and helpless to resolve our conflict and David seemed to take the side of my sister-in-law. This devastated me and had the effect of distancing me from him for the first time in our nine-year marriage. If at this time I believed in symbolic messages, I would say that God felt our small town and the people in it, including David and myself, were due for a cleansing. For me, the effect of the flood was like washing away everything that kept me feeling safe from the bigger world. But like Jonah in the whale, I was soon to be spit out of what I knew as home, family, and community. The flood was the first indicator of major changes in my life but at the time I had no idea just how major the changes were to be.

Months after the flood, when David and I were sitting in our living room, our two children asleep upstairs, he said, "I think I'm going to die young." I replied in the same matter-of-fact attitude, "I think so, too." We spontaneously got up from our chairs, hugged each other, and then went about our lives in the usual fashion. Approximately three months after that hug, David left for a weeklong trip to Michigan. It was February 1973. We were standing at the door awkwardly saying good-bye. I can say this now, but would not have been able to articulate it then. I felt at that moment when we paused at the doorway looking at each other, that if I had said something to David to assure him that I still loved him and that we would be okay as a couple, that David would have come back from Michigan alive. I felt this awkwardness as if it were an entity between us that was waiting to hear what we would say to each other. I did not know that this was one of those pivotal points in time that could have altered the rest of my life. I felt a need to remain silent within myself as if it were a command that I do not speak words that would have been easy for me to speak at any other time in our relationship. It appeared to be the same for David. We both felt awkward. Impersonally kissing goodbye for the last time, he went off saying that he would be home again on Tuesday of the following week. That awkward moment came and that awkward moment left as David went running out to catch his ride and I stood blankly waving goodbye.

A strange feeling of mourning came over me about mid-way through the week of David's trip. I felt heavy inside, almost weighted down. It took a lot of energy for me to make it through the day. At night, after the children went to bed, I flopped on the couch and had little interest in things. And here is what else was strange; I began sleeping on David's side of the bed. This was something I had never done before when he was away and although I was aware of this being different, I did not think too much about the changes in my feelings or habits. Since the flood in June, and the breakdown in communication with my sister-in-law, I already had new emotions that I was not used to and this seemed to be more of the same. There is more. On Sunday night around eight-thirty, I was lying on the couch in my now usual heaviness but had an immediate need to get up to answer the telephone. The telephone had not rung. I walked toward the telephone, and as I approached it, it made its first indication that a connection from outside was intruding into my living room. At the second ring, and without being surprised, I answered saying a simple "Hello."

"Is this Roseanne Schaller?" a stern voice asked on the other end.

"Yes."

"Is your husband David Schaller?"

"Yes." I replied automatically as if I weren't really there.

"Does your husband reside at 22 South Elm Street?" the unemotional voice continued.

"Yes" my automatic-robotic voice came back once again in response to his question.

"Your husband died on the operating table at 8:05 tonight. He had a car accident and crushed his chest when he ran into a stone abutment around six o'clock."

In the most astonishing way, I replied with the following, "Would you please call his mother for me, as I don't think I can tell her." He agreed and I proceeded to give him the number. That was it. I was just as remote as if the person on the phone had called to tell me David's tools were found at the bus station or something as unimportant as that. How did I become so capable of receiving this information and so clear headed to know that I could not be the one to inform David's mother? Of course, I did not remain clear-headed. After some time went by, I began to cry, then I began to wail with heart wrenching sounds until my five-year-old daughter came down the stairs peeking at me through the wooden slotted railing. When I saw her peering through the railing, I was shocked back into the awareness of my role as her mother and I hugged her and eventually told her that her Daddy had left us and gone to heaven. As if she were now my peer instead of my daughter, we cried together hugging each other. "He said he would never leave me," she cried. David kept his word and did return home on Tuesday. His body was delivered and funeral arrangements were worked out. I was now David's widow. It was the early seventies. Women's liberation was in full force. President Nixon was going through his Watergate impeachment trial. People were fed up and rebelling violently against the Viet Nam war and against the hypocrisy of the leadership of the country. One day I was completely enclosed in a safe environment with support systems buffering me against the intense and immediate problems of our world, and within a few short months, I had joined the world in all its pain and confusion. I was raw, open, and vulnerable.

In March, almost two months after David's death, my parents babysat my daughters and I took a much-needed rest by the Gulf of Mexico with my friend, Debbie. The mind amazes me. All day long she and I were lying between the sand dunes protecting us from the cool wind while trying to sunbathe. I had been listening to music on a portable radio. The announcer reported the date; it was March 28. How many times I heard the announcer report this date, I can't tell you. It was many times throughout the day, but I didn't take it in. Later in the evening, Debbie went to the picture window which expanded the width of the room and which looked out onto the Gulf of Mexico. The ocean waves undulating in the darkness seemed to take on a violent foreboding expression. Then I realized that this day would have been David's thirty-third birthday. Debbie started pulling on the drapery drawstrings closing off the roaring ocean and foreboding darkness. "I can't breathe," I panicked. "I have to get out of here." I ran out the door and down the stairs onto the cold sand. I had an instant awareness that this was night, that it was dark, and that there were no visitors yet in the cottages around us. Ordinarily I would have been self-conscious of my next behaviours but this night I only knew one thing: I had to run and I had better not stop to think about it. I felt as if I had to run for my life. So I ran, I jumped, I cried, I screamed against the sounds of the roaring waves and into the mysterious darkness. Filling the vastness of the space around me with my noise, I pierced the loneliness that I felt deep inside of me. I roared back at the bleakness and at the point of confusion that seemed to be housed in my body and penetrating my mind. I ran, I jumped, I cried, I screamed and then I stopped. I conquered something. I knew that I had conquered something. I was no longer feeling pursued by this force that propelled me out through the door attempting to engulf me. I conquered the energy that had welled up inside of me and I stood there as if I were standing in the eye of a tornado. I felt the roaring dynamism around me. I became the dynamism. I became the undulating dynamic meaning of life. I was the meaning, I am the meaning, and I am the point for which the whole planet exists. Me. I was no longer afraid or confused. The darkness of the night seemed to move and breathe. The stars vibrated as if they were not just dots on the black cloth behind them but were ornaments of celebration. The ocean waves were no longer frightening and foreboding but seemed to be trying to obtain my attention and approval. The whole world around me was there for my pleasure, vying for my attention. At that moment, I stepped onto my spiritual path but did not understand the path or what being on a path meant. I knew that this was a beginning for me and that I would make the rest of my life's work understanding the experience. I became a seeker."

The Water element is heavier than Fire and Air and its movement is downward. Water reacts to the ideas of Air and the actions of Fire. As it reacts, it stimulates our imagination and assists us in assimilating our experiences. This assimilation helps us to take these experiences into our Earth element so we can begin to store memory. The Water element strives to bring feelings to the surface. Water element people often hold back and fail to test the waters in the real world. This holding back is often due to their fear of being laughed at, thus, they diminish their reflective powers for stimulating imagination and creative pulses.

Meditating on the banks of the Ganges

PATH MARKER #3 -- REFLECTION

Expressing your emotional body is vital to your spiritual journey. Feeling and expressing emotions takes courage and conviction and is an ongoing process of self-discovery. If you do not claim your personal power (fire), you will not have a strong identity (air). You will, therefore, not be solid (earth), but will be constantly shaping and adapting to the will of others (water). A rich emotional life brings sensitivity and love for the struggles of others and an ability to have intimate relationships.

I BECAME A SEEKER

As we grow in awareness, we have to decide whether we will claim our place on the stage of life. The Water element in us deals with how much visibility we want with others. Here we deal with our relationship to choice. Here dualistic pulls are evidenced as we are pushed and pulled with decisions about re-creating ourselves by joining forces with others for mature personal and professional relationships.

In I BECAME A SEEKER, I lived in my own little world before David died. As long as I did not have to take responsibility for my actions by living in someone else's shadow, I was not fully engaged in living my own life. Jung says that, *"It comes about that when the mere routine of life in the form of traditional conventions predominates, a destructive outbreak of the creative forces (i.e., the archetypes) must follow."* [8] When my Fire came forward at the age of twenty-seven, I was not well adapted to feelings of anger, frustration, aggressiveness, or fear. I was more comfortable placating people, making their needs more important than my own. After David died, I quickly angered, telling people where to go if they got in my way. I went on a rampage of satisfying my own needs often at the expense of others. I simply did not care anymore what the world thought of me and if the people around me did not like it, they could leave. I had an outbreak of creative forces that left me feeling manic-depressive. At one instance, I could conquer the world and at another, I was paralyzed by fear that the world would destroy me. I watched these swings come and go and over time, I noticed that the swings became less in their amplitude as well as less in the degree of expressions. I watched these swings as an observer as I was already a well-developed observer of others, constantly on the lookout for "safe" people that I could trust. I noticed that it took a year for these swings to adjust themselves to what I supposed were normal for mature adults. As I suppressed my emotions while growing up, the distinctions for appropriately using them were not lively activated in me. We do not want to go through life having everything be okay with us. This is like a primitive person not making distinctions about the world in which they live. To evolve beyond the need for everyone to approve of us, we must trust our own experiences and validate them by bringing them out to be shared with others. A Water element person must be careful not to let the influences of others dictate what happens to them in their life. Once David died, I gave myself permission to let life propel me outward and

---

[8] C. G. Jung, The Integration of the Personality, trans. S. M. Dell, Farrar and Rinehart, N.Y. 1939 p. 195

forward testing the waters along the way. We must take our place in the physical world of matter. We must trust enough to re-act to the world we live in, giving expression to those reactions and letting the Water-element in us so beautifully teach us how to expand our emotional range.

THE INSPIRATION TO CREATE

Forced by a traumatic situation to experience my emotions, I was reborn through the element of Fire. This rebirth assisted in my accessing and developing my Air, or the clarity of what I wanted to be and do in this lifetime. Fire liberated an explosion within me releasing the emotions welled-up from years of suppression so that I could begin creating real boundaries (Earth) through conscious discernment of what was appropriate for me and what was not. Without feelings, the inspiration to create and re-create is dampened. Feelings enrich our lives and stir deeply within us a longing for more entertainment of feelings and a desire to experience new things. Einstein said, *"Imagination is more important than knowledge."* How the Water element serves the holistic pursuit is to ensure that re-creation, or varied use of all the elements takes place. By being an interface and catalyst for the other elements, Water helps in joining the inventiveness of the mental or Air element, which cannot produce but can invent, with the fiery focused energy of the Fire element, which does not reason, but has answers.

The Water element, often lacking in ideas and new processes for problem solving, reacting to Air and Fire, strives to co-operate through a harmonizing of these elements thereby preparing the elements for mixture with the element of Earth. Water assists in coming up with the most creative suggestions for processing results. When the first two elements are joined and connected to Earth through Water, catalytic responses bring imaginative expressions into any environment -- something newly invented (Air), by a novel (Fire) and highly imaginative (Water) process is manifested (Earth).

ASSIMILATION TAKES TIME

Water element people have to assimilate the process by absorbing the experiences into and through their bodies via their feelings. In order to transfer their experience into the physical world of matter, time is needed to interpret the feelings. The Water element person, because of this assimilation process, does not function as quickly as Fire and Air, which are lighter and faster processes. Until feelings can be interpreted, the concepts of the Air element will be missing many distinctions. These distinctions are enlivened through our sensate bodies, providing real world evidence. This evidence can be measured in the physical world through an understanding of the processes involved as Water has to communicate with others in some way, such as art forms, gossip, or dramas, in order to assimilate their experience.

SELF ANALYSIS

 Through self-analysis, the individual soul uses the elements of the personality expressed through the body to enliven itself and fulfill its desires. Through our feelings we register the distinctions required to adjust the process of moving ideas toward manifestation. A divine discontent in the seeker keeps the seeker on the path as they make distinctions about themselves along the way. Through their pursuit to holism, the Water element assists the seeker in tapping into and using all the elements available in their human instrument in more imaginative and creative ways. Dr. Mishra says, *"Know this: Mental and natural powers are looking to you to give you something that you have never seen before. They want to enrich you with divine and eternal powers. Eternal forces are serving you constantly, whether you know it or not."* [9] By serving spiritual energies, we ask, *"How can we wisely use our feelings for enriching life?"*

---

[9] Ramamurti S. Mishra, M.D., Fundamentals of Yoga, Lancer Books, Inc., New York, 1969, p. 56.

CATALYST – WATER – REFLECTION
IMAGINATION AWARENESS
DEVELOPING FLOW

To develop imagination, proper use of the expressions of feelings is necessary which is developed by the following postures in the metaphysical Svadisthana or second center of awareness located in the abdomen area.

Resting on your tummy, begin the Cobra Pose by placing your palms flat on the floor just under the shoulder joint. Keep your arms and elbows close to the body. Imagine your shoulder blades are touching in the back. Inhale and slide your nose, chin, and chest off the floor using your hands only for support. Using mainly your back muscles with your arms for support, look up toward the ceiling thereby stimulating your pituitary and pineal glands. Feel the tension in the back as you tighten your buttocks and straighten your legs. Hold until you are uncomfortable. Exhale and lower yourself slowly to the floor leading with your chest, chin, nose and forehead. Pause. Next, go into the Locust Pose by resting the forehead or chin on the floor and placing your fists along the sides of your body. Inhale, and lift your legs up toward the ceiling. Hold until you are uncomfortable. Exhale and lower your legs. From here, move into the Child's Pose by hinging the buttocks backward onto your bent knees. Rest your head on the floor and relax. Feel happy and safe as a child in the womb of the mother. Relax and breathe.

SUMMARY OF THE WATER ELEMENT
FOR SPIRITUAL GROWTH

Reflection of life and its mysteries make you somewhat of a seer of the unseen. An unending supply of divine expression flows from your receptive cup as your imagination leans towards the mystical.

When maturely developed, an abundance of creative expression is channeled into the arts, healing, or in any field where you can transform negativity through the laws of give-and-take. Co-operation and harmony are keywords as you strive to live a life dedicated to peaceful co-existence. Your generous and versatile nature draws people to your calm atmosphere. You can reflect and bring practical applications of the secrets for a happy life with others.

When unbalanced, you can be secretive and live a life behind a veil, masking your true feelings and confusing those around you.

Overindulgence in sensual pleasures diffuses your creativity while overly sensitive reactions to the judgement of others bring about depression and a withdrawal from life.

CAPTURING COGNITIVE INSIGHTS
WORKSHEET

By serving spiritual energies, we can ask, *"How can I wisely use my feelings for enriching life?"*

_____

_____

_____

_____

_____

_____

_____

_____

_____

_____

_____

_____

CHAPTER SEVEN
Elemental Psychology
THE EARTH ELEMENT
PATHMARKER #4 "DISCERNMENT"
Using the understanding of Earth for Discernment, we develop wisdom through our experiences in the world. We strive to conserve our energies while completing our tasks and handling our responsibilities in our families, on our teams, with our colleagues, and with our clients.

YOUR WISDOM, DISCERNMENT AND YOUR RESULTS

A NOTE ABOUT THE EARTH PROFILE AND STRUGGLE STORY

The following profile and struggle story may be too detailed for some readers and they may find themselves bored with the content and lose interest in it. This is exactly the point of the profile. The Earth-dominant person is interested in the many details and although the details may be too much for some of us, the strength of the Earth person rides on their ability to focus on the many details in a project. Earth people are not always appreciated or even recognized for their contributions as often we experience them as too critical, too detailed, too methodical, which could be experienced as too focused on reality. Yet, this is the gift -- a real recognition of how to take care of the things of the Earth by conserving and replenishing resources.

THE PURPOSE OF THE EARTH ELEMENT

The Earth element deals with the aspect of our conscious existence. Through a sense of order and the use of reason, awareness of the finite material world is provided. When dealing with our first Chakra energies, we are dealing with our actual physical bodies, our feelings of security and safety, and our place on Earth. When balanced, the wisdom of the Earth element stabilizes us ensuring responsible wealth is manifested.

Muladahara -- The Base Chakra
The Element of Earth

 The first Chakra at the base of our spine grounds us and represents our connection to our place on the planet, our sense of security, and our fears of loss of physical stability. Here the struggle is to understand and use wisely the material world for producing, manifesting and creating results without wastage or overindulgence. The modern attitude, Jung asserts, *"entirely forgets that it carries the whole living past in the lower stories of the skyscraper of rational consciousness. Without the lower stories [Earth], it is as though our mind is suspended in mid-air. No wonder it gets nervous."*[10]

---

[10] C. G. Jung, Psychology and Religion, Yale University Press, New Haven, 1938, p. 41

HOW TO FULFILL THE NECESSITY OF THE EARTH ELEMENT

The Earth or physical element provides us with the foundation to carry out our tasks. Informing us of our limitations and parameters, this element acts as our critic as it tries to give us feedback when we are "off course" or have gone too far in one direction or another. If we are without too much awareness of the Earth element, we may lose touch with the limitations of natural resources and create too many pie-in-the sky schemes that leave us feeling ungrounded and uncertain about where we are going or what we are doing. The Earth element holds memory, experience and draws on the wisdom from the past for solving problems.

Bill working on his scientific instrument.

THE EARTH PROFILE

Bill is a person who prefers the Earth element. He always has a solid sense that he has a place in the world. He enjoyed the structure that his parents provided for him and although they rarely expressed themselves emotionally, he always felt he was loved.

In his words, *"I felt this security through the consistent behaviours that my parents displayed. I came to count on regularity, calmness, quiet, and a congruent sense of where things belonged and how things fit together. I was a child who preferred to think things out before acting on anything. Sometimes I may have thought too long before acting but I had to sort things out in my mind first before I felt I could move on any thought. Once I had things figured out, I then felt secure in my approach to tackling a project or an assignment. My social side was not very vast, having few friends as a youth. Although they were few in number, I was, and still am, a loyal friend who attempts to stay connected over the years. There may not be many telephone calls or get-togethers but there certainly will be the odd post card, email, or letter from me. I don't have to hear from others in order for me to remember them. I just have a sense of being connected with them.*

I received degrees in mathematics and physics although I preferred physics to math. I think I took my mathematical mind as far as it wanted to go before I was able to move on to physics as a major. When I think about it now, these studies make sense to me as a person geared toward the Earth with a connection to the Air elements and less oriented to either of the social profiles. Physics, because it explains the physical world to me in a way that I need to understand it, and mathematics, because it helps put order in the world around me. Some people may find me boring as I neither express my feelings very much nor do I tend to take the initiative to start things. I tend to be a person who goes about my business, seeing what needs to be done, doing it, and being quite content with working on projects where my talents and abilities are useful to others. That does not mean that I can't be creative or sociable, it just means that I may not notice those things that deal with human interactions and may have to be reminded to do things that others would know to do, naturally. Once I do notice what is socially required by others or someone may have reminded me to notice, then I quite enjoy myself when doing social things and hope that others enjoy being with me.

Because the physical world and its orderliness mean so much to me, I try to honor it when and wherever I can. A demonstration of this was raising our children; I always tried to teach them to put things back where they belonged. The shopping carts at the grocery store belong back in the line up of carts and not left in the parking lot, for example. When there are candies by the cash register in restaurants I told them to take one maybe two, but not a handful. If we had guests over and drinking or smoking took place in the evening, I always liked to empty ashtrays and throw away any bottles from the night before so it didn't leave a negative impression on a new day. When you take out the garbage, wrap it up carefully before discarding it. Be sure to take special care of broken glass in the garbage so that the people who have to pick it up will not be hurt. Wrap it carefully in a container so that there are no sharp edges sticking out. Don't be too loud; never play music so loudly that it would disturb the neighbor's peace and quiet. Shovel the snow from the sidewalk and be sure there is no ice, in case someone should slip. Follow the rules so that there is orderliness for one and all. Do the best job you can at what you are assigned to do. Don't skimp on details or take shortcuts, as you'll probably find that if you do, you have made more work for yourself. You may as well take the time to do it right the first time. In thinking this way, you will actually conserve energy in the long run. I often find that I am willing to do the jobs that others may have little interest in doing but which give me the satisfaction of completion.

My mission on this planet is, I think, to ensure that ideas are manifested through tireless and methodical approaches. By taking in the information through the five senses of the body (taste, touch, sight, smell, and hearing) you can process the ideas and ensure that they are fully developed because you are dealing with concrete, tangible data and real parameters along the way."

WHAT ARE WE MEASURING?

When we interpret our world predominately through our Earth element, we are measuring things that have real parameters with limitations in finite matter. When we use the holistic approach, we tap into the whole system not just the segregated parts of the material system. In the pursuit of holism, we want to consider the physical parameters as well as the spiritual qualities for uplifting the human spirit toward harmony and beauty.

Applying the information to a broader view of life, we must consider our decisions and the impact of those decisions on the system as a whole while satisfying, tempering and developing our own individual needs. Since much of our day-to-day awareness deals with getting around planet Earth, conditional things, things of the Earth make it appear as though we are meant to make only self-centered choices. It is the job of the individual on a spiritual path to transform their self-centered desires into the desire for uplifting and fulfilling the soul's purpose. This is accomplished by becoming a channel of the life force from above by using the human instrument for the creation of ideas in the material world. In doing this, we assist in the creation of 'Heaven on Earth'.

When we measure our results, we need to know what we are measuring. Are we measuring our results from a competitive, finite, human analysis where *"I win, you lose"* or are we measuring how much humanity, compassion, and forgiveness we are contributing to the world, where *"nobody wins if somebody loses"?* This does not mean that we become everyone's doormats. Rather, this means that we learn what is happening in our own experience, become clear about the feelings that need to be expressed (social), analyze the situation (physical), and create ideas that produce inspirational results for the whole situation (mental). If that means that you give feedback that is difficult to say or difficult to receive, then that is what is required. But be conscious and understand clearly what you are after and the consequences of your thoughts, words, and actions before you initiate them.

When dealing with our place on Earth, the personality is dealing with its relationship to the opposing forces of fear versus safety, or how secure we feel in the world with others. When issues around security are not dealt with, then we will continue to be offered opportunities for breakthrough, breakdown, or break with the old. Our work with the Earth element also deals with our connections to our original family of father and mother and how we felt about their authority over us. Here we may deal with the fear that there is not enough to go around, there may be a lack of trust in general and a need to feel in control. Or, we might feel that we are too secure in our world and tend to get complacent. Here we expect that things are the way we think they should be because that is the way they have always been. We become too set in our ways and reduce our ability to be flexible and adaptable to an ever-changing world.

THE EARTH STRUGGLE STORY

IN SICKNESS AND IN HEALTH

I had never had a girlfriend before, but I knew that we would be together. Since I'm not a person who makes instant decisions, the decision to marry Natalie was not one that I took lightly. It took me two years to ask her to marry me. I wonder now why she waited for me. She had a delicate nature and was sensitive to the feelings of others and the world around her. She had a creative inclination and satisfied this need through painting abstract pictures, landscapes, and copying other artists' work. She seemed so delicate that I felt that if I were to hold her too tight, I would bruise her. Natalie's background was one that lacked stability. Her parents had gone through the war and they had suffered from the turbulence of the times. Often they were afraid for their lives. More often than not, they lacked enough food required for a growing family. Emotional stability was also lacking in Natalie's background. Raised in a family environment of conditional love, emotional warfare between father and mother, sometimes different father figures, the household confusion and stress was deeply felt by Natalie. She became the emotional container for the family, feeling all the feelings that could not be dealt with verbally by the adults. My world was unfolding as I had planned it and after marriage to Natalie, which took place in Holland, we went to Canada where I finished my Ph.D. in space science. One evening, a colleague of mine from Malaysia, came to dinner. He knew something about palm reading and like most people, we asked him to explore what our palms had to say. As a scientist, I certainly did not give much credence to the reading. "Your palms show that you will have two important relationships. The second relationship lasts longer and the person is stronger emotionally." I, of course, dismissed this because it simply was not possible. Then he read Natalie's palm and he told her that she had a fork in her lifeline and that she would be coming to a major decision point in her life before she was to reach her thirtieth birthday. If she made her decision one way, she would have a short life. We put this reading behind us after our colleague left and blissfully lived out the next few years while I worked on my thesis.

Once finished with my graduate work, Natalie and I moved to Ottawa and I took a temporary job at the Observatory. That year Natalie gave birth to our son. Natalie seemed to be making her adjustments to our baby and I helped in the evenings. Life seemed stable enough and, and as I had planned it, the following year we went to Paris where I worked as a project scientist for two years. I wanted to experience more of the world before settling down to building a pension and to a job that required a long-term commitment. We took the occasional weekend trips exploring Europe together and I thought we were quite happy. I developed an interest in learning about and trying new wines. Together we developed a few close friends from our neighborhood. Once again, we had adjusted ourselves to life as we led it in Paris, to each other, to our son, and to the plans I had outlined. As I felt strongly that our son should grow up in an English speaking world, after a couple of years in France, we returned to Canada. I took a university position as a project scientist, designing instruments for measuring the upper atmospheric winds. The location of the university was Downsview, Ontario, which was situated in the northwest end of Toronto, Canada. It was the early seventies and Downsview was still a new suburb of Toronto. This meant that there was not much around our area except the university, storehouses, industrial complexes, and a strip mall or two. Downsview was extraordinarily dull and bleak after living in Paris. In retrospect, of course, I can see when the problems began. I did not, however, have the capability to understand them at the time, let alone know what I should do to make things better. I did take note that Natalie had stopped painting. She also did not seem relaxed and she started to become increasingly distant. In my limited understanding of women, I took this to be normal for a new mother. Since I had always been a person who would not feel comfortable interrupting others or imposing my needs onto others, I felt that if Natalie needed to stare out the window for long periods of time then she must have a need to do so. So, I left her alone. Natalie continued to be remote and I began taking up more of the unfinished household chores in the evening, as she seemed too tired to do too much during the day. I thought that she must have been going through quite a lot, as it was also during this time that she became pregnant for our second child. In the first few months of her pregnancy, she seemed happy. I was again hopeful that we would be as we were when we first got married and that having this baby would make everything right for Natalie. On the good days when Natalie seemed like her old self, I placed a lot of hope in thinking that we were okay and that things were normal. These "normal" times came and then diminished as I began leaving work earlier and earlier, worried about our now active five-year old son and about how Natalie was coping throughout the day with him. Somehow, I persuaded Natalie to go to a doctor to see if there was something that he could do to make her feel more relaxed. After her examination, we sat facing the doctor together and Natalie shared her inner turmoil for the first time. She said she was hearing voices and that they were telling her what she should or should not be doing. The voices seemed malevolent and she had to struggle to deal with them and struggle to keep some footing of her own thoughts when dealing with the voices. This, understandingly, made her quite exhausted. The doctor told us to go home for the weekend and that she should come back on Monday. At that time, she would be admitted into the hospital for observation. She was into her eighth month of carrying our second child, another boy. It was during one of the two evenings of that weekend as I was reading to our son that Natalie kissed each of us on the forehead, stroked our hair lightly, and told me she was going upstairs to visit a friend, and that she loved us very much. I felt ill at ease and thought I should see where Natalie was going. I put the book down and told our son not to move but to wait right there until I got back. I walked out the door of our apartment and looked up and down the corridor looking to see which direction she took. I did not see her and so decided to look in the stair well. I looked up and saw that she was sitting on the ledge of the windowsill with her feet dangling out. I instinctively knew that I should not make any sound as I quickly ran up the stairs hugging the wall trying to get to Natalie without scaring her. My mind was crystal clear and all I wanted to do was get close enough to her to grab her and pull her back inside. Although I ran quickly up the stairs, it seemed as if I spent a lifetime on each step. Just before I could reach her, just seconds away from her, she pushed her body off the ledge. I was left standing at the window looking at her body as it floated down the three stories of our building to the ground level. I again hugged the wall as I descended the stairs but this time I was not clear headed. I was dazed as I heard my voice shouting her name over and over again. "Natalie, Natalie, Natalie." Other people came out and were gathering around her as I ran up to her. Taking her hand in mine, again I realized how afraid I was to hold her too tightly in case I might bruise her. She was still conscious as she looked up at me. " Oh, Daddy", she cried, "what have I done?"

Although Earth has a great deal of patience and longs to nurture us, if neglected and taken for granted too long, can sabotage and de-stabilize us throwing us back onto ourselves. We are forced then to return to our roots to learn again and again how to appreciate the simpler things in life. The Earth element is heavy, solid, and tangible and unless mixed with Water, not moveable without a great deal of effort. Secure and stable, the Earth provides us with a sense of our place in the physical world of matter.

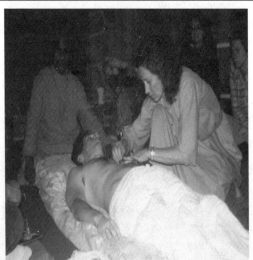

**Bill getting an acupuncture treatment from
Dr. Saraswati with Dr. Mishra looking on.**

PATH MARKER #4 -- DISCERNMENT

Be aware of your need to over control your life. You may not see, feel, and hear important data although it is right in front of you. The need for too much control will certainly limit your actions and opportunities. Without any control, however, we are like a house without a foundation.

TOO MUCH STABILITY
HINDERS ADAPTABILITY

We see IN SICKNESS AND IN HEALTH the social connectors were not enlivened enough to take advantage of new data which would have stimulated new ideas and new actions, new feelings, and different results. Earth was stuck within itself and was unable to adapt to the demands of the situation. The story demonstrates how being rooted in the need for controlling one's life (so much Earth) prevents a person from seeing new things and thereby making different, perhaps more appropriate decisions. The story unfolded without much use of the connectors of Fire, (using new problem solving processes) and Water, (discussing and drawing out the feelings, reflections and reactions of self and others). Water, by discussing feelings and re-actions, would have loosened the solidness of Earth or one's position about the situation. And Fire would have learned from Water (emotions) that new problems were being brought to the surface to be processed and resolved. Fire would have been able to generate new approaches and actions due to the frustrations to find a solution to the current reality. Air would have had to come in and change the belief systems of the individual by coming up with a new idea of the principles that would provide an overview for driving a new way of thinking and behaving.

When the need to control the events around us is too great (Earth), tension in our overall inner and outer system will require something to give, creating an unstable system. It is not easy to know how much stability (Earth) versus instability (Water because of its fluidity and Fire because of its lightness) any system requires or can handle at any given point. I once worked with a colleague who started her own business while working as a medical doctor and a director for a walk-in doctor's clinic. She also had three children and a husband with whom she did not get along. I asked her why she did not leave him and she responded, *"because I just couldn't handle one more thing."* If we do not pay attention to the data and feedback around us, we cannot make responsible adjustments.

In Bill's 'struggle' story, IN SICKNESS AND IN HEALTH, he had a preponderance of the Earth element and for his own personal soul psychology, the life lesson, though very painful, uprooted him from his sense of himself and his need for physical stability and control of his world. As long as he held onto that understanding, he would be living a life holding onto his need for a self-determined form, for self-control, and for self-preservation at the expense of evolving. If Water and Earth can mix well then Earth can easily get the data it needs to actually manifest the ideas of Air and solve the problems using the force of Fire. Unlike the other elements, the Earth element gets its satisfaction from the actual building of the idea. Earth may say, *"We only have so much time to produce this idea. I know from past experience that we have to do the following measurable steps and in the following manner in order for us to get this done on time and within budget."* Of course, no one wants to hear this and thinks that the Earth element is an old 'stick in the mud'. Having an innate sense of time and space, Earth often thinks that there is some foolishness in the Air, Fire, and Water elements. Earth, however, continuously goes about doing its job, getting very little acknowledgement for doing so, but is committed nonetheless to ensuring that the ideas actually are manifested on Earth and within Earth's real time and space limitations.

A beautiful example of the tensions that can cause a system to destabilize in order to recreate a new expression of that system was demonstrated in the drama involving Princess Diana in the Royal family. For the whole world to see, the drama of their lives unfolded before our very eyes through the following expressions.

AIR -- Prince Charles, spoken of as aloof, abstract, and detached, appears to prefer the mental Air element. For him to learn how to relate to others in the mundane world, he had to be forced off the mountaintop down into the world where the rest of us live, expressing our lives through our feelings and interactions with others.

FIRE -- Fergie, spoken of as spontaneous, fiery, impulsive, and reckless, appears to prefer the social Fire element. Forcing us to re-look at the serious and pompous life of the Royal Family, she poked fun at the system and stirred things up to be reviewed.

WATER -- Princess Diana, spoken of as warm, caring, sensitive and subjective, appeared to prefer the social Water element. She attempted to deal with social injustices within the Royal Family by giving expression to her many feelings. She wanted to bring the Monarchy into the 21st century by making it a Monarchy 'for the people'. She became England's "Queen of Hearts".

EARTH -- The Queen, however, appears to favor the physical, solid and stable Earth element, held onto the very stable expressions and hierarchy of the Monarchy.

Through the struggles of Diana processing and sharing her feelings publicly (the social expression of Water), combined with Fergie's actions which appeared to poke fun at the Monarchy's pompous ways (the social expression of Fire), the Queen (Earth) was forced to reconsider how she ran her Monarchy. As a result of setting up a marriage between Charles, who was in love with someone else, and Diana in order to gain heirs to the throne, Charles remained distant and aloof (Air) but tied to the royal system. He did not, however, take into consideration how this marriage would impact other peoples' lives -- especially a young starry-eyed lady. The real symbolic event, culminating the whole drama of this breakdown and breakthrough with the old system, was the castle catching fire. The Queen was forced through these tremendous struggles to till the stolid Earth and loosen her somewhat outdated ways of representing the Monarchy. She began to pay taxes and expressed publicly her feelings as she spoke of her struggles, thus, becoming more human to her public.

When hierarchical systems on Earth are not dealing with the current needs of people and the resources required to satisfy those needs in appropriate ways, then forces begin to operate to "waken" the system. In this way, hierarchical systems can continue to evolve rather than be destroyed. As we struggle with our environment to create a stable, secure world, we must, at the same time, be careful not to be too stuck in this need as instinctual forces will oppose too much stability and will create some chaos by stirring things up. We can continue to evolve by developing all our capabilities and tapping into the whole system within us: the mind, the body, and the feelings. Carl Jung said, *"the individual ego [Mental-Air] could be conceived as the commander of a small army in the struggle with his environment [Social-Water] – a war not infrequently on two fronts, before him, the struggle for existence [Physical-Earth], in the rear, the struggle against his own rebellious instinctual nature [Social-Fire]."*[11]

WISE JUDGEMENT

To tap into your spiritual self at the Base Chakra, you need to use good planning, wise judgement in the use of finite materials, and a practical determined approach in carrying out your plan. The Base Chakra, the Muladhara, is your foundation for creating form, shape and substance. This foundation is developed through orderly progression and careful assessment when putting the pieces of any situation together to create a whole. A wise and responsible use of the material world and its resources is demonstrated in the wisdom of, *"if you take care of your money, it will take care of you."* To evolve as an "awakened" person and be responsible for our life on Earth requires not only the appropriate use of the resources of the material world, but wise judgement and in our pursuit of holism. Dr. Mishra said, *"By the power*

---

[11] C. G. Jung, *Psychology and Religion*, Yale University Press, New York, 1938.

of knowledge and discrimination, you will be able to know truth and untruth; reality and unreality; purity and impurity; immortality and mortality; righteousness and unrighteousness; pleasure and pain; knowledge and ignorance; the Self and the nonself; light and darkness, etc. By knowing them, you will begin to mold your life in the light of the first in the pair and you will renounce the second. When the second in the pair, that is to say, impurity, unrighteousness, etc., are removed from your life, happiness and peace will dawn in the mind."[12]

To spiritually express our Critic, and to develop useful discernment, we can ask, *"What are my fears?"* By bringing our fears to the surface, we look at the inner small self and the feedback required to address these fears responsibly. We then ask, *"What can I do to address my fears and achieve a secure place in the world while also nurturing and protecting the resources of the community?"* For example, once a client of mine paid me for a large invoice with checks that bounced. I noticed that this was causing me to lose sleep and I was constantly pre-occupied with fear and anger. I asked myself what the fear and anger were about. The answer came that I was afraid we would not be able to cover our current moving expenses. I also realized that the anger was from my wanting this money so much that I gave my power away to this person. I did not feel that she was trustworthy in the beginning but I chose to overlook that feeling because of the financial need. Knowing what these feelings were trying to tell me, I then set about asking myself what I should do now to solve this problem. I discussed this with our bank manager and he

---

[12] Ramamurti S. Mishra, M.D., Fundamentals of Yoga, Lancer Books, Inc., New York, 1969, p. 205

very quickly extended our line of credit. Stability was back in my life and my world was back on track. Without the feelings and lack of sleep, I may not have addressed the financial situation as soon as I did. By not addressing the tension, I may have lost more sleep and soon my health would start a downward spiral. Who needs that? Certainly, I knew better than to let run-away fear dictate how I lived my life. Ask yourself these types of questions and record your answers. Then, turn the answers into the action items of the Realist for moving forward on your spiritual path.

CRITIC -- EARTH -- RESPONSIBILITY
AWARENESS DEVELOPING FLOW

To develop discernment at the metaphysical Base Chakra level, perform the following:

Sit in a comfortable, stable position with the spine straight and your hands resting on your knees. Begin the journey into a meditative state by focusing on your breathing. The mind needs somewhere to place its attention in order for it to cooperate with the process of meditation. You will notice thoughts. Just notice them, do not do anything with them. Just notice. Continue to focus on your breathing. Without any attention on the end result, sit silently in this manner for 10-15 minutes. Now, slowly, carefully, stop the process of focusing on your breath; wait a few seconds as you register your attention back to your awareness of the body and how it is sitting in the stable upright position. Now, lie down for 2 minutes registering the peace and silence you felt in meditation before going back into activity.

Take this peace and return to this state again at your next sitting. Once in the morning and once in the evening is all you need to begin to feel the connection of your self with your higher Self, that which is connected to the spiritual realm of all possibilities.

SUMMARY OF THE EARTH ELEMENT FOR SPIRITUAL GROWTH

 The solid and stable energy of the Critic ensures the production of our wealth and our sense of security that are so vital to a peaceful and happy life. The Critic who is methodical, thrifty, and practical uses responsibly grounded energy as slow and steady progress is made to acquire wealth.

When balanced, work and leisure go hand in hand as the mature individual respects the values of the material world for conservation, production, a wise use of resources, and a deep concern for the welfare of the community.

When unbalanced, energy is undeveloped in the physical awareness and a person lives above the laws of the land, the expression of this energy is slovenly, with no honoring of the parameters of the physical world. These patterns create wasteful habits that bring undesirable associations, debt, loss, and suffering.

When these energies are too focused on the physical side of life, we might work only to accumulate more money and more possessions. Stimulated by the need to hoard everything for ourselves, we amass a bigger share of the pie becoming greedy and selfish and not very interesting people.

CAPTURING COGNITIVE INSIGHTS
WORKSHEET

By serving spiritual energies, we can ask, *"What can I do to address my fears and achieve a secure place in the world while also nurturing and protecting the resources of the community?"*

_____

_____

_____

_____

_____

_____

_____

_____

_____

_____

_____

_____

CHAPTER EIGHT
Become Your Own Sage

The journey of pursuing holism is like climbing a mountain. One step at a time eventually gets you to the top, but not without a great deal of effort. Sometimes we make it to the top, and sometimes we do not, but the journey is always exhilarating.

Starting an ascent to higher levels of consciousness, the  individual attempts to integrate the experiences of life. Driven by a divine discontent and using nature's gift of the personality, the seeker taps into the intelligence of nature's elements of Air, Fire, Water, and Earth to slowly shine the Inner Light of the spirit through the human body. This is accomplished by the seeker reaching upward in their vision while building downward through their efforts.

THE SPIRITUAL-HUMAN JOURNEY

For understanding our personal soul psychology we have used the framework of visualizing the elements of Air, Fire, Water, and Earth as an equilateral triangle consisting of our Mental Side, our Social Side, and our Physical Side where each side of the triangle is equally important to the whole. Air represents our thoughts and where we place our attention from our mental side. Fire and Water represent our connections with ideas, people, and things using vigilance and reflection from our social side. And we register and record our experiences in our bodies through our Earth element from our physical side. Using these sides of the triangle, we begin our journey to higher levels of awareness through the expressions of our personal soul psychology to incarnate soul (being) into matter (personality expressions coming through the body). Certain steps, however, can assist us on this journey:

Step one -- Firstly, that we identify our God-given tools each of us has as a physical expression of the mature distribution of these elements that is naturally ours. For example: the mature Air expression using its Dreamer qualities of vision, softens the dualistic tendencies of the first three lower Chakras enlivening within us the expression of purity and compassion. The mature Fire expression using vigilance enlists the aid of others bringing ideas out of the realm of concepts into actions of service in the world. The mature Water expression using reflection channels an abundance of creative emotional expressions transforming negativity through the laws of give-and-take and co-operation. And the mature Earth expression using discernment wisely uses and replenishes the material world for the good of the community.

Step two -- Secondly, we begin to work with the resources for creating 'Heaven on Earth' by using our gifts in ways that allow for expanded expressions of our thinking mind. We do this by learning to take a broader overview of the events in our lives and move beyond either-or decisions that are restricted by conditional results. By tapping into and wisely using all four elements within us, we consciously work on the process of developing our personal soul psychology. This conscious approach expands our awareness of these elements as we objectively observe and analyze our intentions, interactions, and undertakings with others. After all, what most of us are after is peace and happiness. *"Peace and happiness are all manifestations of the higher Self. All material states that give peace and happiness are like the moon, because they reflect the light of the Self; but the Self is the source and the sun of the external light of peace and happiness. When the sun rises, electric lights, moonlight, etc. fade away. In the same way, when spiritual peace and happiness dawn in the mind, all material peace and happiness fade away before it.... Peace and happiness are the end of material life because all living beings live for peace and happiness. In the ordinary state, the mind has identified itself with matter; therefore, it is called material mind, but in spiritual practices, it identifies itself with the supreme; therefore it is called the Self and the Spirit."*[13]

UNIVERSAL ENERGY AND PERSONAL SOUL PSYCHOLOGY

The challenge for each of us is to ensure that the ideas, or visions of the Father (Air), are fully integrated into matter represented by the Mother (Earth). The opposing forces of the Father and the Mother provide creative tension. This dynamic tension between the interplay of Earth attracting or magnetically pulling on the element of Air activates the dance of life. Wisdom of life comes from combining both the originality of the Father combined with the wisdom and experiences of the Mother, thereby expanding awareness of our limitations

---

[13] Ramamurti S. Mishra, M.D., Fundamentals of Yoga, Lancer Books, Inc., New York, 1969, p. 206

and parameters. Wisdom is enlivened through the constructive interactions of the two interfaces of Fire and Water, referred to as the social principle, with that of the Mother and the Father. Without these connectors interfacing from above to below, the amount of information permeating our system is limited. It is like a trinity at work: the Father (Air), the Mother (Earth) and the interfacing of both through the children (Fire and Water) produces something new. Without the interfacing of the social connectors, our decisions would be limited as Earth and Air have different properties. How can they mix? Think of the play of life as "boy meets girl." The boy (Air) and the girl (Earth) are attracted to each other and start to look for commonalties and how they can get along with each other (Water). However, once they are used to the commonalties, they want to be recognized for their differences (Fire) and strive to give expression to these differences. These differences either strengthen the relationship or cause the relationship to break down. If they are aware that this is a natural and healthy process, the differences will become complementary, and the maturity of the couple's expression and intimacy will grow and produce quality results. Each part of the play of life is necessary for production and reproduction of new expressions of life.

DEVELOPMENTAL FRAMEWORK OF PERSONAL SOUL PSYCHOLOGY

Personal soul psychology gives us a way of viewing our lives. For developmental work using this framework, we bring our natural gifts forward while at the same time becoming increasingly aware of the need to develop the less preferred elements, those elements that are not so preferred or natural to us but have to be accessible when we need them. These elements used in the pursuit of holism must be accessible to us for balancing the over-developed more natural element as well as to completely develop a holistic system within ourselves. If we do not access them and develop our least preferred awarenesses or elemental expression, they will remain dormant and inaccessible to us and we will be less effective in our pursuit. We do not want to surrender our natural talents or elements to the other elements, but we do want to be able to call upon them and enliven them as required. We can picture our development with others as follows using a standard teambuilding model:

MATURE RELATIONSHIPS

$\times$ **TRANSFORMING**
Now we transmit our mission outward.

$\times$ **PERFORMING**
Now we fully express ourselves (Air-learning/growing/sharing).

$\times$ **NORMING**
Now we strive to get along with others as we create some new rules or norms to live by (Water-Earth/assimilating/cooperating/affiliating)

$\times$ **STORMING**
As we grow, we strive to be recognized for our talents (Fire-power/ego/will). At this stage, we see our differences.

$\times$ **FORMING**
When we get together with others, we strive to get to know each other, looking for similarities (Water-affiliation), we strive to get along. We also hold back a bit because we do not know if we can trust each other (Earth-security/safety).

MATURITY OF RESULTS (vertical axis)

MATURITY OF RELATIONSHIPS (horizontal axis)

In the forming stage, we are not producing great results nor do we have mature relationship patterns. In the storming stage, we have moved up the scale on results and strengthening relationships as we strive to maximize our talents with and through others. Most people stop their development at the storming stage of life not wanting to confront issues or recognize and work with people's differences. Here, the will or Fire part of us is called on. Without the will, we stay dependent as children hiding from our own growth and evolutionary process not pushing outward to test the waters.

This developmental growth process of living and working with others is not static. It changes when new variables are added to the situation in which we find ourselves. Up and down the maturity developmental scale we go: sometimes more mature, other times less mature -- but we learn more about ourselves at each stage. We must bring our issues to the surface and learn to create rules and procedures that honor individuals, family members, and teams. Creating rules and procedures is the norming stage. In order to operate at high levels of maturity, we must establish some norms to follow and boundaries to honor.

One way to develop our clarity and conscious use of the elements is to refer to Abraham Maslow's, the industrial psychologist, hierarchy of needs. Maslow said we could not aspire to higher needs until the lower needs have been satisfied. We can pose a question to the mind that will assist us in understanding our needs by asking, *"what are my needs or motivation and intention when dealing with this person?"* Using the four lower Chakras for consciously working with motivation theory, take 100 motivational points and distribute them across four basic motivators (elements) and see what you consciously want from each interaction. Ask yourself, "do I want to play it safe and put my 100 motivational points on security issues (Earth) because I am dependent on this person but do not trust them? Do I want to make friends and be liked by this person or this group and put my 100 points on affiliation and cooperation (Water)? I know I will be compromising and accommodating but perhaps making friends is more important to me right now than exercising my will. Do I want to be recognized for being different and unique, so I will put my 100 motivational points on power (Fire) although that may mean that some people *some people will not take well to this? Or do I want to learn more from this person in order to stay objective and resolve the issue in a constructive manner (Air)? I may not get my way but I will not compromise on the results either.*

Never distribute your 100 points across all four motivators, elements, or Chakras as this will only confuse the process and will lead to mixed messages. After your interaction with the other person or people, distribute your 100 points again to see how you did. This will tell you what was driving your behaviours and how the process affected you. There are times when you must exert your will and other times when you may need to back down. The important thing here is that you do what you do consciously and accept the consequences of your own decisions. This is a very simple technique and I use it all the time to understand what I am after and how I should proceed. For example, if I have been driving too fast on the highway and I see a police car behind me with the flashing red lights telling me that I am being pulled over, my lower Chakra, related to security issues, will most likely be stimulated and I will distribute my 100 points as follows:

0	100	0	0
Fire/Power	Earth/Security	Water/Affiliation	Air/Learning

Since I know that I am in the wrong, I will play it safe and take what is coming to me by withdrawing into myself and being cautious and guarded. I do not need to make the officer my friend nor do I want to exert power over him/her. This would be foolish. I really do not have to learn anything about the situation as I already know the speed limit and that I was wrong.

If, on the other hand, I am going to a party with people that I like and want to get along with, I will put my 100 points on affiliation.

0	0	100	0
Fire/Power	Earth/Security	Water/Affiliation	Air/Learning

By being clear about your conscious intention or motivation, the mind automatically comes up with the strategies it needs in order to evolve and learn how to develop and access the other motivators. All motivators or elements are important for growth. Once we are operating at a high level of consciousness with our interactions and situations with others, then we begin transforming our mission outward on a more regular basis -- serving self, others, and projects with maturity.

There is a story of a disciple who was on a boat crossing a river with other people. The other people were discussing his guru and running him down. The disciple did nothing to counteract their bad mouthing of his guru. Later on when the guru heard about this, he gave the disciple a strong scolding saying that he should have had enough respect to stand up to these people and defend him. Another disciple crossed the same river on another day and people on the boat were badmouthing the guru that day. This disciple yelled at the people for bad mouthing him. Later when the guru heard this, he scolded the disciple and told him he should be more humble and learn to accept people for where they are.

All the disciples became confused by their guru's different comments and asked him, *"why were you mad at the one disciple for not speaking up for you and then you were mad at the other disciple for speaking up for you?"* The guru said that the lesson was opposite for each disciple -- one needed to be stronger and the other needed to be more humble.

Becoming conscious about our motives, what we need to learn and develop, and how our actions create our results are important in our evolutionary processes. If we do not deal with our lives in a conscious way, nature will provide us with lessons to wake us up.

MANIFESTING 'HEAVEN ON EARTH'

To manifest 'Heaven on Earth', we can think of Air as light energy that expands upward toward Ether. Fire, as one connector that transforms Water into gas also expands upward toward Air. Water, as the second connector that transforms Earth into a liquid form, moves downward. And Earth, as a downward flow of magnetic energy, consolidates the elements into form. All of these elements could look as follows:

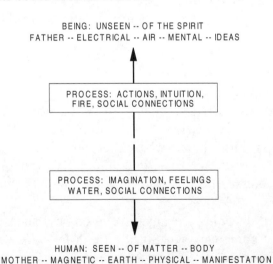

BEING: UNSEEN -- OF THE SPIRIT
FATHER -- ELECTRICAL -- AIR -- MENTAL -- IDEAS

PROCESS: ACTIONS, INTUITION, FIRE, SOCIAL CONNECTIONS

PROCESS: IMAGINATION, FEELINGS WATER, SOCIAL CONNECTIONS

HUMAN: SEEN -- OF MATTER -- BODY
MOTHER -- MAGNETIC -- EARTH -- PHYSICAL -- MANIFESTATION

When viewing our soul's work using this structure, it appears as though we have a number of aspects working within us. We have the aspect of Spirit, which we cannot see and we have that part of us that is matter, which is of the Earth and is tangible or seen. The Earth part of us comes from the word "human" which is from the Latin root humus, meaning *of the earth* and is tangible and visible; while the unseen, 'Being' part of our "Human Being" selves is of the Spirit -- our essences, our character, our moral compass. We use the great elements of Air, Fire, Water, and Earth to bring our ideas out of the realm of concepts (Air) and convert them to physical realities (Earth).

DEMANDS AND PRESSURES SHAPE OUR LIFE

When we review our lives, we see that we are often presented with situations that place significant demands and pressures on us to make decisions about "who" we really are. Every decision we make impacts our life and eventually determines the course our lives take, thus, shaping our character along the way. These demands and pressures use our three main awarenesses as follows:

1.   MENTAL -- The awareness of how we think about things, or our mental awareness. This awareness deals with our expectations and perceptions of the way we see the world. We refer to this awareness as Air, which is unseen and is everywhere. It can be felt, especially when it is a strong wind, but it is unseen, spacious, light, and uplifting. Air can become destructive if not respected thus creating hurricanes and tornadoes that can destroy.

2.   SOCIAL -- The second awareness of where our demands and pressures come from is the awareness we

experience from the differences of people with whom we associate. The people we associate with, what we do with them, and how we connect with them, can be referred to as our social awareness of Fire and Water. Fire heats things up and Water can dampen things. Both elements can, like Air, be destructive if not used properly. Fire, when not attended, consumes. Water, when not honored, drowns us or becomes stagnant and polluted.

3. PHYSICAL -- The third awareness where demands and pressures come from is our backgrounds, our histories, and our memories. This awareness draws on our home life, our hometowns, the events in our lifetime, and the projects on which we work. This awareness also draws on how we are registering information through our sense of smell, sight, taste, touch, and hearing. This registration of information is used as feedback. This sensate feedback is designed by nature to teach us to honor and respect our limitations, to work within the constraints of the physical world, and to increase our wisdom of how to work more efficiently and effectively through the conservation of energy and matter. In the physical awareness, we store and stock memory of the things that we do, thus saving us time and energy in processing future similar data. When not tended to, Earth can destabilize us through earthquakes.

To pursue holism, use the mental aspect of yourself by asking the mind to participate in bringing spirit into matter. We take into account the finite nature of the physical plane but also rise to a higher mental space by asking the question, *"How can I serve myself and others in this situation?"* This question allows the mind to join in the pursuit of holism with the body and spirit by automatically looking for ways to contribute. By this intention alone, we can begin the process of incarnating the higher expression of the soul's purpose coming through the physical form on earth. We combine the expression of our higher spiritual self with our lower or Earth self, which is connected to the finite nature of the material world. Our mind begins to realize that it is not losing its hold on the body and appreciates being asked to participate in producing finer and finer results. We use our connectors on our social side, Fire and Water, to look for and connect to the people and resources required to serve higher purposes. Here we have to be clear of our motives and intentions no matter with whom or what we do. This takes some analysis and is an ongoing process of looking for meaning and understanding.

Sometimes we are required to stand up for something and take a power position (Fire) and other times we may be required, like the second disciple in the story above, to take a back seat and try to get along with people and not overpower them (Water). Other times our intentions may be to learn more about the situation and remain objective (Air), while at another time we may need to take a safer position with a situation because it is too dangerous to do anything else (Earth). We need to analyze and be clear in order to proceed with our development as well as for the good of the whole.

There are times that we will not be able to understand the purpose of our actions until later. We still need to be clear even though acting without understanding the overall purpose of a situation makes it more challenging. In this case, we have to trust that there is something grander at work than meets the eye requiring that we live with ambiguity until we understand.

Using our physical awareness is where the rubber hits the road. When we take responsibility for the results we produce in life, we use the physical parameters to convince our higher Self that we mean what we say. It is not enough to say, *"I take full responsibility for these results,"* unless we are prepared to pay the price of what that means in terms of real money, real time, and real effort -- not just words or thoughts but also actions and follow through. If we give our word and fail to follow through and others pay a price because of us, then according to cause and effect, we must pay them back in like form. Pay them money or pay off a debt through some effort. But saying, *"I take responsibility for this,"* does not make it so until we put real physical actions behind our words in order to convince our spirit that our human side (matter) is wise and not making a mockery out of our words. As Jerry Seinfield said in one of his episodes where he reserved a car at the airport but when he got to the airport, there was no car available, *"Anyone can take the reservation, it's <u>keeping</u> the reservation, that's the important thing."*

Many people would rather shift the blame and look outside of themselves for the culprit when things go wrong. However, in pursuing holism, we realize we are responsible for the actions we take or fail to take. To demonstrate that we are responsible, we must be willing to have our word mean something in the physical world. When we are prepared to be responsible for our life in the physical world then our life has to turn around. This is a very important part of the process of pursuing holism.

STORYBOARDING THE ELEMENTS

Storyboarding, used for organizing and planning for filmmaking processes, can be used as a process for organizing our ideas and how to manifest them. If we storyboard the four elements and awarenesses, we would see that they take the following form:

The Air element in us provides us with sight and can see and initiate new ideas and ways to view things. Because Air is spacious, light and everywhere, it is unencumbered by details and feelings. It is also not interested in the actions required to fulfill its own ideas. Air is interested in initiating new ideas and our first storyboard would look like this:

THE IDEA

Fire comes into play next and wants to connect the new idea to some actions thus beginning the process of bringing the idea into reality. Focusing on solving the problem of kicking the idea into reality, Fire acts "as if" the idea is possible and begins an iterative process of trial and error moving the idea forward by connecting it to whatever resources it has available at the time. Similar to the Air element, Fire is not that interested in cumbersome details or getting caught up in emotions that could slow the process of moving the idea forward. It is also not that interested in the actual building of the idea. It is predominately interested in forward movement, which provides the heat or friction necessary to cause the idea to manifest. Fire gets us involved by stimulating our energy and motivating us. At this level of the production of the idea, the Fire element because of its upward movement, can go up to the mountaintop (Air) where it can see clearly the original idea and remind us of the reason why we are doing something. Then using its natural urgency to solve problems comes back down from the mountaintop refocusing our attention by connecting the idea to the next set of actions and moving the idea forward. Fire takes one or two steps forward and then adjusts its actions as it confronts new problems or friction along the way, heating up its experience by continuing in this fashion. Our storyboarding at this point might look like this:

THE IDEA

THE ACTIONS

Next, the Water element comes in and says, *"Wait a minute. You are not considering the impact of these actions on others and on me. I don't feel right about the process or how quickly the steps are being taken."* Having said that, Water proceeds to do a consensus with everyone else involved asking, *"How do you feel about this?"* Checking out the process of manifesting these ideas through the actions taken by Fire, the Water element goes around gathering data about how people are reacting to the process and the whole idea in general. This checking out process can often be challenging for Water, as it can question and at the same time feel guilty about questioning and hurting Fire but it wants to ensure social justice for all. In the questioning process, Water is also concerned that others may interpret its process as gossiping.

During this stage of the manifestation of the idea, however, the storyboards now look like the following:

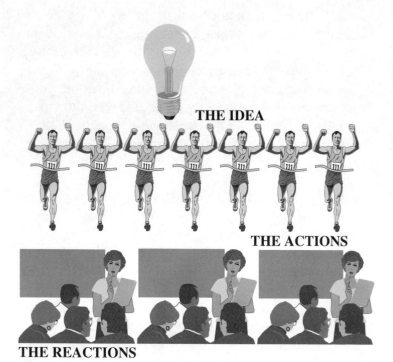

THE IDEA

THE ACTIONS

THE REACTIONS

At this stage in the production of the idea, things could look a bit muddled when mixing the idea, actions and feelings with Earth. Water is trying to mix the ideas from above downward into Earth or matter. It does this for two purposes, firstly to assist in the manifestation of the idea of Air and secondly to slow the speed and reduce the friction generated by Fire. By doing this, things will not burn up or burn out before the results are evident and the formation of the idea is in a tangible form.

By slowing the process down, assimilation of the idea into matter begins to take shape. The Earth element by its thorough attention to details along with its deep understanding of limited parameters involved in producing any idea, ensures order by aligning all the details, actions, and reactions of the group in a systematic way allowing the idea to be finalized, take form, and be manifested.

Using the connectors of Fire and Water, ideas coming from the mind or Air begin to be shaped into matter and now our thoughts are not just good ideas without substance. The Earth element, drawing on past experience and through the physical calibrations of taste, touch, sight, sound, and smell ensures that our results are tangible, measurable, repeatable, and useful. By use of our overview (Air), our actions (Fire), our reactions (Water), and our physical calibrations (Earth), feedback is provided which increases our ability to integrate all four elements until the results we are after are completed. Thus, by the manifestation of ideas on Earth, we have the opportunity to create 'Heaven on Earth' and our storyboard now looks like this:

THE WHOLE SYSTEM AT WORK GETTING THE JOB DONE WITH, THROUGH, AND BY PEOPLE

THE IDEA-inspiration

THE ACTIONS-process

THE REACTIONS-process

THE TANGIBLE MANIFESTATION OF THE IDEA-form

BECOME YOUR OWN SAGE

When we use our diverse gifts and talents in ways that inspire positive constructive results, seeing the planet as a whole system, we begin using not only our sight, but we also use our 'insight'. Insight is our capacity to understand hidden truths and comes from our ability to develop the powers within thus becoming our own sage. We become our own sage when the intellect is honed and taps into the complete systemic knowledge when and wherever it is required. To tap into the complete systemic knowledge takes a clear mind (Air), a strong will (Fire) committed to human service, a vivid imagination for creativity to blossom (Water), and a commitment to listen to, build on (Earth), and feed the facts back to the mind. This is true reasoned inspirational intuition, connecting and inter-linking all aspects of our personalities in human form with our higher Self in appropriate ways. This insight becomes our finest teacher: our finest hearing, our finest touching, our finest seeing, our finest tasting, and our finest smelling -- everything we do and say is spiritualized with energy of our higher Self.

When we have digested the information and fed it back to the mind, insight, or developing the powers within, allows us to tap into and develop the spiritual principles of the soul. In doing this, we not only serve ourselves but we serve the whole planet by incarnating soul into matter. Insight allows us to oversee a finer level of the intellect for expressing ideas, developing healthier relationships, and producing finer results.

THE ELEMENTS AND THEIR
PSYCHO-PHYSICAL EXPRESSIONS

When we use the elements of life as the three awarenesses of mental, social, and physical in the Chakra System, we can view the dynamic interplay of these elements as a prism that can refract white light into its component colors. If white light metaphysically represents Universal Consciousness, we can extend our analogy to view the human instrument as the instrument of refraction. If the human instrument of refraction, like a prism, is cloudy or not made of clear material, then the light rays being refracted will not be clear but will bleed into each other.

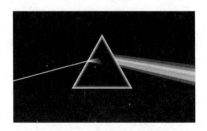

The colors, metaphysically linked to the Chakras, can enhance our understanding of the elements and the various attributes of human expression. Using this perspective, we can look at how our individual personalities and the patterns, both balanced and unbalanced, express themselves. For example:

THE FOUR LOWER CHAKRAS

 AIR -- ANAHATA Chakra: In the Yoga Chakra System, Air is the color of green and is esoterically related to the chest area in the body helping to purify the inner atmosphere with the outer atmosphere.

BALANCED AIR EXPRESSIONS

Air is fast, light, all around us but unseen. Air provides us with our potential for creating new things within a space or atmosphere. By trusting in itself its values and beliefs, it learns to give expression to, and create beauty and purity around and within us. The element of Air relates to the archetype of the Father and has the continuous job of initiating or creating something new. The archetype of the Father is responsible for clarity and our sense of identity, or who we think we are and where we place our attention. Air being gaseous, allows us to ascend upward.

PSYCHO-PHYSICAL UNBALANCED AIR EXPRESSIONS

When Air is unbalanced, however, it stirs things up and we have confusion, an overdeveloped sense of ourselves, or a loss of our identity or sense of who we think we are. When Air is unbalanced, we might have problems with our throat, with the use of our voice, our breathing, with our heart, or any part of our neck and chest areas. We may also get headaches because of neck and shoulder stiffness. If we could see this with a metaphysical eye, we would see that the color green is now not clear and is polluted with a mixture of other colors giving confusing messages.

 FIRE -- MANIPURA Chakra: The element of Fire is esoterically related to our solar plexus area in the body and activates our metabolism and digestion. It is the color of yellow and provides the energy, power, and force to take our ideas into the world and confront the challenges along the way.

BALANCED FIRE EXPRESSIONS

The element of Fire is related to the archetype of the Warrior. It is the job of the Warrior in us to give us power and force. The Warrior, using power and force, generates friction and heat which allows us to refine our developmental process throughout our journey. Just as heat evaporates water into an active gaseous state, Fire activates us moving us outward and upward. The frequency of Fire, like Air, is also fast and light but can be seen and felt. As we confront our challenges in the real world with and through others, we develop confidence, improve self-esteem, and gain a stronger sense of who we are through our day-to-day actions.

PSYCHO-PHYSICAL UNBALANCED FIRE EXPRESSIONS

When Fire is out of control, it becomes self-absorbed and burns itself and others up along the way. When this happens, it no longer has the capacity to light the way for new actions but destroys or burns everything in its path. When unbalanced, we experience indigestion, acid stomachs, and changes in metabolism. Metaphysically looking at this Chakra, we would see that the color yellow is polluted by other colors, thus causing a variety of dysfunctional actions.

 WATER -- SVADISTHANA Chakra:
Located esoterically in the lower abdomen area of the body, Water is associated with reproduction, circulation and the mixing of energies. Water is associated with the color orange and is related to our ability to join things together.

BALANCED EXPRESSIONS

The Water element is like the archetype of the Judge. Water has a dissolving effect turning solids into liquid. When balanced, Water develops a strong sense of integrity ensuring that honoring of the self takes place. The frequency of Water is slower than that of Fire and Air but not as dense or slow as Earth. Water teaches us about justice and how to develop a social conscience. As we go about speaking our truths and listening to and honoring the truths of others, Water attempts to blend and harmonize everyone in the world and, moving in a downward flow, mixes ideas into the physical world of matter.

PSYCHO-PHYSICAL UNBALANCED WATER EXPRESSIONS

When polluted, Water creates feelings of despair, murkiness and darkness. When unbalanced, problems with relationships exist and problems with circulation, reproduction, or sexual expression can be present. When metaphysically viewing this Chakra, the color of orange is muddied and relationships are poorly managed.

 **EARTH -- MULADHARA Chakra:**

Located esoterically at the base of the spine, the Muladara Chakra is the color of red. The Muladara or Earth element deals with our abilities to bind materials together and manifest something tangible in the world.

BALANCED EARTH EXPRESSIONS

Thought of as the Mother archetype, Earth represents wisdom developed through experience. When Earth is tilled, tended, and cared for, it is receptive, nurturing, and creates a stabilizing effect as ideas received from the Father, mixed and churned through the elements of Fire and Water, are solidified into tangible realities. The frequency of Earth is slower than the other elements, being bogged down with its own solid mass and weight.

PSYCHO-PHYSICAL UNBALANCED EARTH EXPRESSIONS

When Earth is not tilled and tended, it feels unappreciated. When it is unbalanced, we feel isolated and abandoned without a sense of structure, form, or stability. We might have problems with our bones and those parts of the body that hold and bind us together, such as muscles, tendons, and ligaments. When metaphysically viewed, the color of red is polluted and structures and forms are not stable.

THE THREE UPPER CHAKRAS

Above the first four Chakras in the body are the upper three Chakras. The first four Chakras deal more with our human self, that self that is of the Earth and relates more to the dualistic tendencies of our struggles when living and working with others. The upper three energy centers, or Chakras, represent the following expressions: Ether (how we express ourselves), Conscience (our ability to concentrate), and Intellect (pure energy, calmness, and a meditative nature). These Chakras reside in us as follows:

ETHER -- VISHUDDHA Chakra: Ether is the color blue and is esoterically related to the throat area in the body. Ether deals with our expressions and our ability to take in air, water, food, and ideas. Ether is that part of us that holds the space and is related to the element of Air.

CONSCIENCE -- AJNA Chakra: Our conscience located in the forehead esoterically around the pituitary gland area, is the color of purple. When balanced, we have good equilibrium and good concentration. When unbalanced, we have the opposite effect of poor concentration, a lack of equilibrium, and a loss of balance due to dizziness or confusion.

INTELLECT -- SAHASRARA Chakra: Our intellect is located in the crown area of our head and is the color of magenta. When our intellect is balanced, we meditate with ease, sleep well, and we rarely take in the effects of tension and stress on our nervous systems. We are calm. When our intellect is unbalanced, we feel stressed, cannot sleep well, we become fearful and worry unduly.

PURSUIT OF HOLISM

With increased levels of awareness, we can pursue our lives and maintain a healthy balance of expressions using our God-given tools of Air, Fire, Water, and Earth in the journey of enlivening the soul. As life presents us with various struggles to awaken through the struggles of life, our attention is drawn to unbalances. These unbalances force us to reconsider, to reevaluate, and to re-examine our lives so that we can evolve by increasing our capacity for healthier perceptions and feelings.

The examples of struggles for increasing perceptions and feelings are demonstrated in the 'struggle stories'. For example, in WHO AM I, Bill struggled with his sense of importance and challenged Guruji as a Father figure. This fourth Chakra challenge was taken up by Guruji who addressed the questioner and his sense of self-importance by taking the piece of paper to mean the "idea of this person's own position" and relentlessly addressing the questioner throughout the evening Satsang. The Satsang became an opportunity to teach the lesson of humility and stimulate the Heart Chakra, element of Air, which, when balanced enlivens humility and compassion reducing our need for self importance.

In the story of WHO DID I THINK I WAS, I created an unbalance in the third Chakra and got too full of my own personal power. To correct this and get back in touch with my spiritual path, the overuse of the energy of the Solar Plexus Chakra was brought down by the Earth element at the base Chakra and I got back in touch with my foundation and what was really important to me. I was not meant to be caught up in the material world of selfish interests. My attention had to be turned back to that of service through the loosening of the hold of the artificial importance of money and position on me.

In the struggle story of I BECAME A SEEKER, the unbalance of my second Chakra was that I was emotionally unconnected to the people and events around me. I was not really participating in life and my energies had to be awakened and activated through the third Chakra. Fire stimulated and forced me to make connections between the outer world and the inner world and clarified the purpose of Water, stimulating imagination and re-creation. Stepping onto my spiritual path, I became awake. Instead of being a passive dull reflector of life without an active imagination, I took my place on the stage of life and my energies were activated outwardly and tested in the physical world.

In the story IN SICKNESS AND IN HEALTH, Bill was forced to let go of his need to over control which is an unbalance related to the base Earth Chakra. Here his need to have a too stable world reduced his capacity to deal with the reality that was facing him and he failed to ask questions and to evaluate the situation from other points of view. Perhaps Natalie was mentally sick? Perhaps he should take bolder steps to address the problem? Perhaps the problem is outside of his sphere of comprehending and he should get help?

THE JOURNEY TAKES FORM
THE PERSONALITY AND THE SOUL MERGE

To move into the higher Chakras, according to Dr. Christine Page, *"Awareness of self as part of life on earth transforms into Awareness or Knowledge of Self as part of the Universal Source of Creation. The will of the personality becomes that of the soul."*[14] She goes on to say in her book, Frontiers of Health: *"As the soul becomes more deeply incarnate into the physical form, the lower three chakras receive their higher counterparts and the two energies, i.e. that of the personality and the soul merge."*

Enlivening our spirit requires that we take responsibility for our own expressions in the use of the elements both balanced and unbalanced. To actively move into the higher Chakras, we can ask the question, *"Will I make decisions that enliven my spirit or will I make decisions that debilitate me? I know that decisions based only on the lower Chakras deal with conditional relationships to self and others. What can I do to elevate my attention, increase my vigilance, stimulate my imagination, and create meaningful outcomes for everyone?"*

MATURE AND IMMATURE EXPRESSIONS

Sometimes we try to take a shortcut by having expressions around us without developing them in ourselves, e.g., by marrying someone who expresses these qualities. When we do this, we do not grow. Moreover, the very person we were attracted to for those

[14] Christine R. Page, M.D., Frontiers of Health, The C. W. Daniel Company Limited, Essex, England, 1992, p. 90.

qualities start to get on our nerves. We then, in some unconscious way, draw the people and the events to us that force us to expand: usually through a struggle, a crisis, or a breakdown of the relationship. We then return again to the second Chakra to repeat the pattern with another person.

EFFECTS OF IMMATURE OTHERS ON US

When a person is too much Air we experience them as unrealistic in their expectations of us. Always living in the overview without a realistic sense of the detailed physical world, Air preferred people are forever escalating their demands to achieve greater and greater results, never appearing satisfied. We can soon grow tired of this. Losing our self-esteem around these people, we move away as we can never reach their ever escalating and unrealistic requirements. To stand up to this person requires that we be clear about the problem that their behaviours have on us and to articulate this problem in a way that respects them, the outcome, and ourselves. If this person is unwilling to work with us on the resolution of this problem, then we best pull away.

When a person is too much Fire we often experience them as too intense and dominating, causing too much friction and discomfort. When we are around a person who is moving too fast, we either speed up our own processes or we burn out. Exhausting to be around for any length of time, we tend to move away from the immature Fire person because we feel that our needs will not be honored. Once again, we should strive to inform this person of the impact of their immature behaviours on us in an objective and thoughtful manner. We always speak of their specific behaviours as the problem for us and never use a statement that can put them down. For example, we can say, "when you speak loudly, it triggers in me a feeling of being wrong and then I find it difficult to speak up for myself. Can we work out a method of communicating without raising our voices so that I can stay engaged with you on this project?"

When a person is too much Water, we experience them as overly sensitive, taking everything too personally and bogging us down with all their processing of feelings. When around an immature expression of this element, we soon grow tired of having to walk around on eggshells and tend to want to avoid this person, looking for someone more stimulating and productive. Explaining to this person that spending so much time around their feelings is causing us to lose our focus in getting the job done often goes a long way to getting them back on track.

When a person is too much Earth we experience them as holding us back too much when they are stuck in old systems that have outlived their purpose. Tired of beating our heads against a brick wall, we move on and eventually leave this person behind, mocking them for their "stick in the mud" approach to life. Sometimes it can be difficult to turn the Earth person's position around but we should strive to speak to the value of changing their position and not label their behaviour as stubbornness on their part.

THE MEANING OF LIFE

With the values of our world changing so rapidly, the need to understand each other and where we as a modern society are going, is crucial. Dr. Ira Progoff wrote of Jung's thoughts on modern society, *"Fundamentally, Jung's diagnosis of the modern man is that he is suffering from a starvation of symbols, a spiritual malnutrition brought on by meanings that became too meager to nourish the soul. Projections and images have been withdrawn from life, and therefore, the world has ceased to seem alive. It is the deadening of images which once had a vital power that lies at the source of the confusions in modern consciousness. The question is whether the occidental people can continue to live as they now are with only a morgue of symbols to supply them with the meaning of life. From Jung's point of view, this is impossible; periodic confusion, paralysis of spirit, and ultimate breakdown are bound to result. That is the negative side, and on the affirmative side is the fact that as a result of the impoverishment of symbols, the psyche must, in time, out of the nature of its inherent creativity, bring forth new symbols from within itself.*[15]

We can be a part of the continuous creation of new symbols by staying consciously awake in order to provide a deeper meaning to our life other than just a material meaning. We wisely use our ATTENTION, VIGILANCE, REFLECTION, AND DISCERNMENT for increasing our spiritual connection as life is of its own importance. 'Above' and 'below', the spiritual and the physical, are equally important. The purpose of life is to wisely use our natural, inherent gifts. The process of

---

[15] Ira Progoff, Jung's Psychology and Its Social Meaning, Anchor Books, Garden City, New York, 1973, p.251.

how we do this and the structures or forms that we build are both important to us, to our families, to our communities, as well as to the *Global Village* in which we must learn to live responsibly each and every day.

Applying Ayurvedic knowledge to living responsibly on this planet, the wise Rishis of India *"took AIR to include both the AIR and ETHER Elements, FIRE to include both the FIRE and WATER Element, and WATER to represent both the WATER and EARTH Elements. The Rishis used this Doctrine of the Three Principles, (in Sanskrit, the three doshas) to establish a healing science which could exist and work in congruence with nature's Law, and which would be broad enough to include all connections of human[ity] with [the] cosmos. This is Ayurveda's holism, the consciousness of the interrelation of all the universal principles.... The origin of these Elements is the Great Undifferentiated Existence from whence all issues, and nothing exists in the physical universe which is not composed of these Five Elements."[16]*

---

[16] Dr. Robert E. Svoboda, The Ayurvedic Press, 1996, Albuquerque, New Mexico, p. 27.

Look to each day of your life and enliven the dynamism of life that we are privileged to experience. Enjoy the tensions and the movement of the expressions of energy for life cannot stand still for one moment. To stand still is not its nature. Look, therefore to this day.

Look To This Day

Look to this day, for it is life,
The very life of life.
In its brief course
Lie all the realities and truths of existence.
The joy of growth, the splendor of action,
The glory of power.
For yesterday is but a memory, and
tomorrow is only a vision, but today well
lived makes every yesterday a memory of
happiness
And every tomorrow a vision of hope.
Look well therefore to this day.

■ *An Ancient Sanskrit Poem*

CHAPTER NINE
What is Yoga?

*From an essay by Shri Brahmananda Sarasvati
(formerly known as Dr. Ramamurti Mishra, M.D.)
Printed with permission of Baba Bhagavandas
Publication Trust, Monroe, New York*

 Yoga means union, the union of individual existence with cosmic existence, union of the individual "I-am" with the cosmic "I-Am."

This union is eternal. You do not have to create it. You cannot create it, because it always exists. You have to feel it. How? Not by an emotional feeling of the thinking mind, but by feeling the original mind, the silent mind with which you are born.

No individual is independent from the rest of existence. We depend on food for eating, on water for drinking, on space for dwelling, on air for breathing. We depend on Nature every moment. As a matter of fact, the individual is in every way the manifestation of Nature. And there is no distinction between outer and inner nature. The universe is like an organic living tree, and the sun, moon, stars, zodiac signs, humankind and all creatures are its leaves, flowers and fruits.

The mind is the world, and the world is the mind. All problems, all wars -- whether individual, domestic, social, national, international, political, religious or economic--are the result of the disturbed mind. Thus, the mind is the cause of our happiness and unhappiness.

What is the cause of the crisis and lawlessness throughout the world? It is lack of union between the body, mind and soul. We need to change our hearts. This is the work of Yoga, which means the holistic union of the body, mind and soul with our heart through love, without regard for caste, creed, gender, color, country, high or low.

Is Yoga a religion? No. What is the religion of earth, water, fire, air, the sun, moon, stars and space? They have no particular religion. They belong to everybody, to the religious and nonreligious alike. Similarly, Yoga is beyond religion and politics. Electricity belongs to everybody, because everyone can use it. In the same way, Yoga belongs to everybody. Yoga is cosmic religion.

One who uses the body and mind properly in time and space, with proper motive for the common welfare of humankind, is the yogi and is practicing Yoga, whether he or she knows it or not. There is no choice between using and not using the mind. There is only the choice between proper and improper use, between unselfish and selfish purpose. One who uses the mind to unite humanity's heart, not only to create unity between the East and West, but to experience that unity with all existence -- he or she is the yogi.

Yoga is the holistic way of life, where union and harmony of the body, the mind, and the soul or consciousness, "I-Am," are fundamental. Accordingly, Yoga has many branches, including physical, mental and spiritual forms and disciplines. In fact, each of life's activities is a Yoga when performed in a natural, harmonious way, attentively, to balance and unite the body, mind and spirit.

What is the difference between science and Yoga? Science deals with objective reality, while Yoga begins with subjective reality and ends in transcendental reality. Science is involved with all types of discoveries and inventions, while Yoga is interested mainly in the discovery of the discoverer, that is to say, the discovery of pure awareness, pure consciousness...the absolute "I-Am." When you have the Self, pure consciousness, pure awareness, then you know the whole universe, objective and subjective, the past, present and future, because you are beyond time and space.

Now our old ways of living are dying, and humanity is searching for the new way. We have the choice between death and life. If we prefer to die, then we do not have to do anything. If we prefer to live, then we have to change our hearts completely from disunity and disharmony to unity and harmony. This transformation is the work of Yoga.

> *BE THE CHANGE YOU WANT TO SEE*
> *IN THE WORLD.* -- **Gandhi**

Following is a summary of questions found throughout the book. These questions invite the mind to work with joining the spirit with matter. You may wish to keep a journal of your observations, the changes in your thinking patterns, and the results in your life.

1. How would I describe how I am living in this world with others? How am I using the resources available to me?

2. In a situation where the fear response is triggered in me, I can ask,
   a. What is really happening here?
   b. What do I want to happen?
   c. How am I contributing to the situation?
   d. What other alternatives are there besides fight or flight?
   e. What can I do differently to contribute in a more constructive way in this situation?
   f. What are my motives -- are they to take power from someone? Play it safe? Try to make friends? Or problem-solve for the benefit of everyone involved?
   g. How can I become more aware of what is motivating me and what I am trying to achieve?

3. Exercise for the mind--Ask the mind to come up with answers to the questions, *"Who am I?" and "Who am I not?"* Just let the mind wander and come up with pages and pages with what it identifies as itself. We get attached to those things we identify with and even think we are these things. In the Depression in the 1930's people thought they were their money and jumped out the window when they lost it. That is how attached we get to those things with which we identify.

4. From the Air element, we can ask, *"what can I do to enliven my spirit and create situations for myself and others to evolve constructively? How can I serve myself and others in any given situation?"*

5. From the Fire element, we can ask, *"what actions should I take in this situation and what are the consequences of my actions on others?"*

6. From the Water element, we can ask, *"how can I wisely use my feelings for enriching the outcome in this situation?"*

7. From the Earth element, we can ask, *"in this situation, what are my fears? What can I do to address my fears and achieve a secure place in the world while also nurturing and protecting the resources of the community?"*

8. To actively move into the higher Chakras, we can ask the following:

    a. Will I make decisions that enliven my spirit or will I make decisions that debilitate me?

    b. I know that decisions based on the lower Chakras deal with conditional relationships to self and others. What can I do to elevate my attention, increase my vigilance, stimulate my imagination and create meaningful outcomes for everyone?

As you work with the Yoga postures and the self-analysis questions, keep notes of changes in both your personal life and the physical parts of your body. For example, when you have a pain in the low back, observe when it started and how it changes as you become more conscious of it as an expression of energy. When the expression of energy gets your attention, by asking some of the questions from the chapters, you can bring the unconscious struggles in the psychophysical aspects of yourself into conscious awareness where you can actively do something with the energy.

Remember that everything is your guru if you are paying attention. Selfless service is the key to vigilant wholesome expressions of higher aspects of yourself. Self-analysis keeps you aware of external forces wanting to serve you and enrich your life, and wise judgement will assist you in the responsible use of the material world. Best of luck on your spiritual journey.

> *"Knowing others is intelligence; knowing yourself is true wisdom. Mastering others is strength; mastering yourself is true power."*
> ■ **Lao Tzu**

To stay vital, here is a summary of the postures you may wish to perform daily:

NAMASTE
A word that means we recognize
the divine in each other.

ABOUT THE AUTHOR

R. Danielle Gault specializes in personal and professional development. She has a BA in Psychology and a post graduate diploma in Human Resources Management. Trained in many natural healing art forms, she was a long-time student of Dr. Ramamurti Mishra before his death. She brings a deep understanding of energy work to her courses in Reflexology, yoga, personality awareness, and stress management as well as corporate programs in teambuilding, problem solving, and communication. She has a great love for teaching and sharing knowledge gained from other teachers. She is trained and qualified in the Myers-Briggs Personality Type Indicator, holistic health practices such as Reflexology, Yoga, Ear Candling, Reiki, and Iridology. She has a MasterTrack in Neuro-Linguistic Programming and is trained in the use of behavioral and cognitive psychological models.

Danielle has worked in the management development field for many years and has acquired a wealth of experience presenting training programs to CEOs, VPs, Managers, Support Staff, and Sales Professionals. This background has provided the basis for her special insights into effective interpersonal skills for enhancing productivity and her thorough grasp of management development initiatives. She has personally delivered programs to a wide range of organizations including companies such as London Life, Home Depot, Unilever, ACE INA, Sprint, Sunoco, and AT&T.

As a respected human resources development consultant, speaker, and trainer, Danielle helps people discover the secrets of achieving personal performance satisfaction through understanding the psychology of interpersonal skills and self-awareness insights.

For workshops and services, please write or call:

R. Danielle Gault
P.O. Box 601
4918 Dundas St. W.
Toronto, Ontario
Canada M9A 4X5

Telephone: +1-416-231-5877
Fax: +1-416-231-5833
Toll Free outside Toronto +1-877-For-Core

Email: coredynamics@cs.com
Website: www.coredynamics.ca

Notes

Notes

Notes

Notes

Notes

Notes